MAKING SENSE WHEN LIFE DOESN'T

The Secrets of Thriving in Tough Times

Foreword by Don Piper

CECIL MURPHEY

Coauthor of *New York Times* Best Seller *90 Minutes in Heaven*

summerside
PRESS™

Summerside Press™
Minneapolis 55337
www.summersidepress.com

Making Sense When Life Doesn't
© 2012 by Cecil Murphey

ISBN 978-1-60936-224-9

All Scripture quotations are taken from The Holy Bible,
New Living Translation (NLT), copyright © 1996, 2004.
Used by permission of Tyndale House Publishers, Inc.,
Wheaton, Illinois. All rights reserved.

Cover Design by Studio Gearbox

Interior Design by Müllerhaus Publishing Group
www.mullerhaus.net

Photo by Veer

Represented by Deidre Knight, The Knight Agency, Inc.

Stock or custom editions of Summerside Press titles may
be purchased in bulk for educational, business, ministry,
fundraising, or sales promotional use. For information,
please e-mail specialmarkets@summersidepress.com.

*Summerside Press™ is an inspirational publisher offering fresh,
irresistible books to uplift the heart and engage the mind.*

Printed in USA.
10 9 8 7 6 5 4 3 2

I've tried to tell true stories in this book, but sometimes
I had to protect the guilty or shield the privacy of others.
When I use a full name, that means I have permission to
tell the story. When I use only a first name it means the
story is true, but I've altered a few facts to avoid lawsuits,
the loss of friends, or disdain from the person cited.

—CECIL MURPHEY

Contents

Foreword

"I don't know if you've heard yet, Don, but Cec's house is burning. If you can get to a computer you can see an online newscast on a local Atlanta TV station right now," the excited voice of our literary agent, Deidre Knight, said on the other end of the phone.

"Oh, no. I'm logging on right now."

In a matter of seconds I watched as the television camera panned across a suburban Atlanta lawn. As if the billowing smoke wasn't shocking enough, the camera's lens came to rest on my friend and writing partner, Cecil Murphey.

Cec was standing in the driveway of his long-time home, his arm draped around Shirley, his sweet wife of many years. As I looked at that dear couple my heart sank. I settled into a deep feeling of sadness and utter helplessness at that moment.

Cec and Shirley lost virtually every possession accumulated in their lifetimes. Even more tragically the life of their son-in-law ended that morning in the flames as well. Irreplaceable photos, manuscripts, memorabilia of their years as missionaries in Africa, first edition books, cars, clothes, everything was gone in a life-altering blaze.

In the subsequent days, friends, fledgling authors that Cec had mentored (and there are legions of them), publishing industry folks, church members, neighbors, and family members poured out lots of love on the Murpheys. Those of us who have worked with Cec immediately collected money for a new computer, without which he could not ply his trade.

But it was a big mess. I'm not certain that Cec Murphey is an expert on messes. I actually hope there aren't any experts in that area. But I do know this: he has experienced enormously difficult circumstances in his long and distinguished life. And what he hasn't experienced personally,

I can assure you, someone else has shared with him. He is a missionary, a pastor, a prolific author, a confidant, a friend, a father, a husband, and a survivor. Thousands of people have poured out stories of their darkest hours to Cec Murphey.

I believe that makes Cec eminently qualified to offer excellent counsel on making sense when life doesn't.

And make sense he does. This book, I trust, will be a classic primer on overcoming the messes of life, a blueprint of how to navigate our lives with the least amount of scars and the most amount of achievement.

For a man who has published more than 120 books, I humbly suggest that this book is some of his best work. You'll find that the words just leap off the page. You'll discover yourself saying, "Wow, that's absolutely true," as you read its pages. Some of Cec's most profound insights are contained in this work. They're not platitudes, but insightful, transparent, sensitive, practical instructions for living a significant life.

Consider his words:

- "I need the empty spaces in life to learn to accept fullness in life."
- "I need my opponents. They often speak the truths that my friends won't."
- "To appreciate others' accomplishments enables me to enjoy my own success."
- "We all have regrets about the things we've done. The biggest regrets are about the things we *didn't* do."

Yes, this is a rich book of wise counsel. I only wish I'd read it when I was at the threshold of my life, rather than on the downhill slope. Yet, I know I will benefit enormously from its wisdom today. And I am supremely confident that you will too.

Making Sense When Life Doesn't is a twenty-first-century template for your most meaningful life. Read! Learn! Enjoy!

Don Piper
December 2011

1

Life Is Messy

LIFE IS LIKE CLEANING THE HOUSE. My wife works hard, and the place is pristine—for a day. Then before we're aware of what happened, the clutter and disorder reappear. We leave things in temporary places and forget them; we spill coffee and don't realize it. The bathroom mirror solicits water stains while dust multiplies in every corner.

That's how life operates, but we have choices.

- We live with untidiness.
- We clean up the mess and wait for the next assault.
- We complain while we find someone to blame for our chaos.
- We decide, *This is the time for me to try something new.* The messes still come—that's inevitable—but they'll be different kinds of disorders.

Take my friend Skip Cothran, for instance, who was a top

wholesale salesman for Oscar Mayer. His job entailed a lot of travel. He and his wife became heavily involved in a local church while she was pregnant with their first child. Skip said to Suzie, "This big campaign will be over in six weeks. After that, I'll have more time for you and our church."

Suzie laughed. "As soon as you complete this campaign, you'll start a new one."

To his credit, Skip didn't argue; he knew she was right.

Maybe you're like Skip. You point to a specific goal and tell yourself, *After I buy the new house, get the promotion, find the right husband, earn a million dollars, or the kids leave home...*

As long as you tell yourself that the chaos and disorder will disappear *when* an event happens or *after* some event, you fool yourself—at least for a time.

Disorder never goes away, because life is messy.

Life will stay cluttered.

You won't escape life's demands.

So how do you react? Changing jobs, moving to a new city, or finding a new soul mate may make everything appear like the pristine house, but your old ways will catch up with you. Maybe you've already figured that out.

Or chaos may have already erupted. *This is the worst time in my life,* you may think. Your company downsized you, you invested unwisely, or your love relationship ended. What then?

- You decide to reside permanently in Disaster City and comfort yourself with the way things used to be.
- You move on because you're forced to make changes— and resent everything that happens.

- You tell yourself, *This can be the best time of my life. I can try the things I wanted to do but never did.*

Life won't ever be perfect, but it can be good. It can be exciting—and even better than you've imagined.

But what if you could make tiny, incremental transformations in your attitude—permanently? What if you could learn to cope with the chaos and move forward so you handle the messes without losing momentum?

In this book, I want to nudge you and suggest ways that you can make your life better. I might have added "in spite of" the hardships, but that's not what I mean. You can make your life better *because of* those adversities. And I want to help you do that.

Life won't ever be perfect, but it can be good. It can be exciting— and even better than you've imagined.

Just so you'll realize this isn't theoretical or suggesting something I don't practice, I want to tell you about something that happened to me in 2007.

Around nine o'clock on a February morning our house caught on fire. My wife and I got out safely and so did our daughter. Her husband, however, died in the fire. The loss of everything else—clothes, furniture, memorabilia, computer, and two cars in our enclosed garage—paled by comparison.

An hour after the fire, my best friend, Dr. David Morgan, arrived.

David hugged me and offered me words of comfort. The first words I said to him were, "I've been preparing for this."

I didn't consciously think of that sentence—it just came to me. But as I said it, I knew it was true. David understood I hadn't expected the death of Alan or the loss of property. He knew I meant that I had been living and preparing to face hardships and losses.

I'd like to help you move in that direction too.

Every time we receive a setback or a disappointment, we eventually work through it—that's how we survive in this life. As the problems get larger (and they do), they nudge us to get going.

If you're introspective, you can look back and think, *I made it last time, and I'll make it this time.* As a serious Christian, I say it this way: "God enabled me to go through the past ordeal; God is still at work and will take me through this one as well."

Sometimes you're wounded, and often you tell yourself, *I hope I don't have to go through that again.* And, chances are, you won't repeat the same problem—if you learn from that experience. If you don't, similar crises will probably keep stalking you.

Try my words. Each time something hits you in the face, say out loud to yourself, "I've been preparing for this." It's not a conscious preparation for disaster, but it means you accept this ordeal as one more mess in your life—and one more mess you'll move through.

Life is messy. I can't avoid the chaos,
but I can choose my response to the crisis.

2

Why This Mess?
Why Now?

THE TITLE STATES THE TWO WAYS I've heard the same question. We seem to think that if we're good people, especially if we're religious or spiritually minded, life will flow rather well for us, and we'll encounter few hardships.

Then, without warning, chaos lands on top of us. Or confusion. Or problems. Regardless of the term we use, we don't like it, and we don't understand.

Asking either of the questions above comes out of our attempt to control life—and we need to get past that silly, futile idea.

The answer to both questions is simple:

I need this mess, and I need this mess right now.

Because I truly believe in a God who is sovereign, I also believe He knows what I need. I know what I want (or think I do), but I tend to opt for the easy, the quick, the expedient. Yet that's not the way I mature as a person.

I want to grow, yet I hate going through the messes of life. We've all heard "No pain, no gain." It works the same way with life as it does with physical fitness.

The messes in life are my best teachers.
I don't like them, but I need them.

3

Finding Our Balance

BECAUSE THE NURSING ASSISTANT had inadvertently left the door ajar, I watched the older man begin his physical examination. "Stand on your right foot for ten seconds," she told him, "then switch to your left."

His compliance caught my attention. He stood on one foot. His arms flapped and his body swayed—forward, backward, to one side, and then the other. He didn't fall, but it was obvious he didn't have good balance.

That's how life is, I thought. *We constantly strive for stability, even though we're not always aware that's what we do. If one part of the body upsets the equilibrium, the rest of the body rushes in to restore the harmony. We might look funny and feel confused, but we do it anyway.*

Life demands balance—and you may look or feel awkward, especially when you're trying to start over and figure out what you want your life to become. Regardless, that's the way life works. Suppose your job required you to carry eighty pounds with your right hand and only thirty with your left. If you carry that load long enough, your right shoulder would naturally bend downward and your left would go up. That's how you'd maintain stability. You'd be balanced, but it wouldn't be good for your health.

You can't see yourself as you really are (no one can). Or, to say it another way, you won't realize when you're truly bent out of shape because you compensate. As long as you have other factors that contribute toward some form of stability, you survive. Or as long as you keep on doing what you've been doing for the past five years, part of you claims, *I can go on this way.* Another part cries out, *This is terrible. Let's make changes and find a better way to live.*

Making sense—good sense—out of a chaotic world constantly throws off your equilibrium and forces you to flap your arms and bend your body in strange contortions. It's not wrong to want to stand with your feet flat on the floor. And the wild contortions may be necessary when you lose your equilibrium through company downsizing, divorce, the death of a loved one, an unwanted pregnancy, financial reversals, or when your kids get into trouble.

But think what happens when you're flapping your arms: it's impossible to solve the dilemmas of life when struggling to keep your balance claims your full attention. That's not the time to make decisions—especially significant decisions.

> It's impossible to solve the dilemmas of life when struggling to keep your balance claims your full attention.

Why not stop trying to keep yourself upright? Lean against a wall, or do something so your arms aren't stirring up the air. It's all right to be temporarily down.

You may need a little time of feeling sorry for yourself. So go ahead and moan over life. Think of what might have been, or how you could have behaved differently. Make it a visit—a *brief* visit—not a place for permanent residence.

This off-balance strategy helps you admit your failure, identify any injustice, and experience sadness, perhaps even guilt, for any role you've played in the event. Too many people want to rush past accepting personal responsibility or feeling pain.

Instead, confront those things. Tell yourself:

- *I was wrong.*
- *I was naive.*
- *I betrayed myself by settling for less than I wanted.*
- *I ignored the warning signs of this disaster.*

Admission is a positive step: it means not only facing yourself before you try to move forward, but also forgiving yourself (and anyone who wronged you). That's why the following principles of 12-step programs are so significant:

Step 4. Made a searching and fearless moral inventory of ourselves;

Step 5. Admitted to God, to ourselves, and to another human being the exact nature of our wrongs.

You can race past facing responsibility, but it will throw off your balance even more. The Christian religion provides a way to deal with our failures. If you don't like the word *failure*, think of *shortcoming, error in judgment, wrongdoing,* or *sin.* Regardless of the word you use, it's crucial to face what you have done (or not done). Confess to God and ask for strength not to repeat your actions. After that, you can move toward a newer, healthier balance.

This also holds a bonus for you. Not only do you forgive, but you learn more about yourself. You identify areas where you're vulnerable or susceptible. You become aware of specific *triggers* or *flashpoints*, so you can avoid the flailing arms and contortions.

I struggle for healthy balance.
I find healthy balance when I face my failures.

4

Don't Waste
a Crisis

FIVE YEARS AGO, I was on faculty at a writers' conference in North Carolina. The director, Yvonne Lehmann, did an interesting exercise with the four hundred or so of us present.

After all of us stood, she said, "If you have never had a manuscript rejected, please sit down." She explained that many of the writers were new and had never tried to get anything published yet. Probably a third of them sat down.

"If you've had only one rejection, sit down." That left a few less standing.

From there she went from five rejections to ten and twenty. By the time she hit five hundred, one woman and another man and I stood. Sandy Brooks said she had received a thousand rejections during her career. Novelist T. Davis Bunn and I weren't sure of our total turndowns, but we both knew they were in excess of five hundred.

Davis and I were probably the most successful writers present. That was Yvonne's point.

After I sat down, I realized I had learned to accept rejections. For the first decade of my writing, each nonacceptance threw me into a depressive mode. By the time I had received two hundred rejections, my emotions had learned to cope. Now I simply shrug and say, "Next time it will sell." It hadn't been easy, but I learned by going through each calamity of a publisher not wanting my prose.

Here's what I've learned. Don't waste a crisis. Learn from it. It's okay to feel sorry for yourself or get angry or depressed—that's normal and natural. But don't let those negative emotions control your life. Instead, grow from the terrible blows. Each crisis you survive prepares you for the next.

It's okay to feel sorry for yourself or get angry or depressed—that's normal and natural. But don't let those negative emotions control your life.

No one likes being rejected. Who likes being fired or reprimanded, especially when you feel you've done your best? A stack of unpaid bills makes you wonder if you'll ever overcome your debts. An illness strikes you or a family member. The death of a close friend or a spouse shatters you. The list can seem endless, but each one represents a crisis of some kind.

Don't waste the crisis. Ask yourself: *What do I need to learn from this experience?* Yes, it's a simple question, but it's not intended to make light of the predicament. You'll survive this crisis—as you have those in the past. You'll also survive the other calamities that will seek and find you in the days ahead, often when you least expect them.

Not wasting the experience means you tell yourself, *This is a life lesson. I need this for my growth.*

You may argue over that last sentence, but it has become part of my personal-growth philosophy. I don't believe in accidents or random troubles. I do believe in a God who is in control of the world—and, specifically, my world. The disasters and predicaments aren't what I would choose, but they present opportunities for me to examine my life. I didn't arrive at this position easily, only after many calamities and catastrophes. When I learned to accept the present disaster and see it as an opportunity to mature and grow, I became stronger and less troubled by the next chaos.

Each time I asked myself the question: *What do I need to learn from this experience?*

I don't always get an answer. Sometimes I understand only years later. Some I'll never figure out. But I know that each time I ask, I accept life's unfairness, injustice, and hardships, and I become strong and more prepared for other crises.

I don't like problems. Who does? But none of us is immune, and surviving each ordeal makes us more ready for the next.

For example, my wife became seriously ill and was hospitalized for fifteen days. I spent large portions of those days with her. At the time I was nearing the completion of a book, which was due the week she went into the hospital.

> This is a life lesson. I need this for my growth.

I had also contracted to write another book (which I had started months earlier). Both were due within a period of four weeks.

Shirley underwent two surgeries and, even after I brought her home, temporarily used a walker and an oxygen tank. The point is that her illness interrupted my work schedule.

What did I need to learn from my situation? The simplest lesson is that my wife is more important than my work. I knew that, but life experiences forced me to make that conscious choice.

Here's another lesson, and it's not the first time I've struggled with it. *Today I have time to do everything I need to do today.* If I can't get everything done I want to accomplish, I'll finish it tomorrow or next week.

I'm highly self-disciplined and expect to finish a project on time—even early. Yet, as I felt the sadness and inner pain of my wife's physical ordeal and knew there was nothing I could do to relieve it, I chose to be with her. Sometimes I did nothing except sit beside her and hold her hand.

As one of my friends used to say to me, "All you can do is all you can do."

I can't choose the crisis,
but I can choose to learn through the experience.

Rediscovering Our Passion

WHEN I WAS ABOUT TWENTY YEARS OLD, John Greenleaf Whittier's poem "Maude Miller" touched me deeply. It's a story of a nobleman and a poor farm girl who meet one summer when he stops at her well for a drink of water. They stare at each other, and both feel love stirring. Nothing comes of their brief encounter because he is of noble birth and she is a peasant. But neither forgets the other and both often wonder what would have happened had they given expression to their feelings.

Near the end of the poem appear these words:

For of all sad words of tongue or pen,
The saddest are these: "It might have been!"

The words had such a profound impact on my life, I determined at that age never to look back and say, "It might have been."

I've made mistakes, and I've taken a few wrong trails—but I regret none of them. Even from those dead-end streets I learned something about life and about myself.

For many of us, life gets in the way of the things we want to do or have some vague hope of accomplishing. Or we convince ourselves that we were immature, naive, or foolish to have such ambitions or desires. Or maybe we don't do anything about our dreams because they seem too difficult for us or impossible to attain.

When I was fifteen years old, I read William Saroyan's *The Human Comedy*. After I finished reading that book, I knew two things. First, I wanted to write. Second, I wanted to write as well as Saroyan. I've since fulfilled the first part of my desire and still struggle for the second.

The problem is that I did give up. At age sixteen, I was immature, inexperienced, and had no idea how to go about becoming a real writer—that is, a published writer. I wrote one short story, sent it to a magazine that didn't publish fiction (which I didn't know at the time), and it was rejected.

After that, life got in the way, and I followed a career path, marriage, and family. But the dream of writing never died. When I was twenty-two, I wrote a nonfiction book and sent it to one publisher. It was rejected, so I threw away the manuscript. I decided I had tried and failed and so I assumed I could never write. The passion that had burned so brightly appeared to have died...or so I thought.

When I was thirty-eight, I tried again—but this time I went about writing differently. I took a class and learned about the craft as well as the publishing business. After totally rewriting my first article eighteen times, I sent it, and it was accepted for publication. My writing career began with the publication of one short article. But, for me, becoming a published author was more than receiving thirty dollars for one full page of a print magazine. It was the time of rediscovering and following my passion.

I've now made my living as a writer for a quarter of a century. My career is more than my success as a writer. It's about *passion*. Before I submitted that article, the fervor had slowly resurfaced—a flickering desire at times, but real. Over the next four years, I had about a hundred articles published. I discovered that words came easily to me, and I wrote quickly. Each time (or so it seems in retrospect) the enthusiasm increased.

When I took the leap to become a full-time writer, I did so after a long time of prayer and soul-searching. I told myself a dozen reasons it was foolish. But I had one major reason for taking the risk: *passion*. My zealous enthusiasm was so strong, I knew it was something I absolutely had to do—even if I failed.

Did I doubt my ability? I had *many* doubts, and they continued for years. Did I think I would make it as a writer? I didn't know, but I couldn't run away from the burning desire to put words on the page. After a prolonged period of self-searching, my zeal didn't diminish. I felt stronger than ever that it was the right direction for me.

Passion has a way of overcoming the obstacles and the arguments. It was something I *had* to do—call it a compulsion. When I stared at the obstacles, I cringed, but each time I faced one, I reminded myself of the words from Whittier and vowed again that I would follow my obsessive desire and never sigh and say, "It might have been."

> Passion has a way of overcoming the obstacles and the arguments.

What would happen if we listened to those inner yearnings, those unfulfilled desires, those deep urgings that whisper, "This is for you"?

It's a good time to focus on inner desires when we reach the place where we are thinking:

- *I've done this before—too many times.*
- *My job isn't fun anymore.*
- *My life is boring.*
- *I don't know what to do now because I don't have a job (or a spouse or...).*

But we need to face the issues realistically, which means with some common sense. I frequently get e-mails from people who say, *I've always wanted to write, and I lost my job, so I wonder if you would help me get started.* Or, *I need to bring in more income. I thought writing would be a good way to supplement.*

What do they really want in my answer to these e-mails? They want me to grab their hands and enable them to leap over the obstacles. Part of the assurance we're doing the right thing comes from facing those formidable obstacles with an I'm-going-to-try-it-anyway attitude.

True passion pushes us to do for ourselves, to search out what we need to do, and to not rely on someone else to do the work for us. It may mean going to school. That's what my wife did. Although Shirley had an undergraduate degree, she decided to go into the publishing field as an editor. She started over again, went to school part time, and earned her journalism degree at age fifty-five.

I can cite numerous examples of the late bloomer. The phrase refers to those of us who never lost that burning desire. But, more important, it means that we finally—*finally*—allowed ourselves to face what we're passionate about once again.

If I follow my passion,
I won't have to lament over what might have been.

6

Old Activities, New Ways

AN OLD STORY BEGINS WITH a student asking his Zen master, "What did you do before you were enlightened?"

"I awakened at dawn, fetched water, and built a fire," the master said and proceeded to tell of the rest of his morning activities.

"And after you were enlightened, what did you do?"

"I awakened at dawn, fetched water, and built a fire...."

The obvious point is that the outward activities hadn't changed, but the inward attitude had. Once we've adoped the new attitude, it becomes normal. That segment of life makes sense—or greater sense than previously—and takes on a deeper meaning. One benefit is that we start to see our crises as things we learn and gain from.

We may do many of the same things, and probably will. The changes will be inward. Or, as my friend David Morgan likes to say, "It's not what you do, but which part of you does it." Our motives change even if we continue to engage in the same activities. Sometimes we will react emotionally (*I feel I need to...*), and sometimes it will be a reasoned statement (*This is my responsibility—or commitment—so I'll act*).

We do some things because we're taught that's the right way, the moral way, the ethical way, or maybe it's what our boss wants done. Once we pull away from old jobs or relationships, we may do many of the same things. but our *reasons* will be different.

> "It's not what you do, but which part of you does it."
>
> —David Morgan

A few years ago, I went through a particularly traumatic time as I dealt with issues from childhood that I had ignored or denied—one of those messy times when life made no sense. Over a period of months, I made peace with my past, forgave myself, and forgave those who had hurt me. I made a number of significant changes—or so it seemed to me. At least *I* knew I was different and no longer related the same way.

Most people didn't seem aware of the changes in me. Perhaps that's because they observed my behavior and weren't perceptive about my motivation.

Two comments stood out. One came from my niece Eldora about an hour after I'd arrived in my hometown in Iowa for a visit. "You're different," she said. "You're quieter than you used to be."

Afterward I thought, *I probably spoke as much as I had before, but I spoke differently. I didn't need to control the flow of the conversation.*

The second came from my wife. One evening we visited a local Greek festival with a couple we'd known a long time. Shirley, standing in front of me, said to Dixie, "Cec has changed so much in the last few months. I used to know what he was thinking or what he wanted, but I don't know anymore."

Shirley was confused; I was elated. She had noticed, and her words verified that I had changed. Though my actions hadn't varied much—I did many of the same things I'd done for years—she was sensitive to my inner changes.

Over time our motives change, our zeal flags or increases, and we spend more time or less time on different projects. The Zen master still went through the same routine each day, but he viewed it differently.

Another example is the transformation of a clerk at our local post office. Usually there are two or three clerks behind the counter. I hated to have one particular clerk wait on me. She was efficient and did her job well, but she never smiled or said "Good morning." *Brusque* was the kindest word I could have used to describe her. I might have been talking to a machine with hands. I once told Shirley, "I feel as if she's doing me a favor to wait on me."

About a year ago, something happened to that clerk—I don't know what it was, and I didn't know her well enough to ask. She's as efficient as ever; she still doesn't make small talk. But now there's a softness in her features, and I don't mind her waiting on me.

Have other customers noticed? I have no idea. She still does the same things she always did, but I believe something positive happened to her on the inside. And to those of us who are aware, she is different.

After I change, I may still do the same things,
but I do them from different motives.

7

Small Failures

"NINETY PERCENT OF OUR DECISIONS and actions are automatic," a local preacher said in a recent sermon. I don't know where he dug up that figure, but I'm willing to accept it.

He went on to say, "We still have options and can change about 10 percent of our behavior."

Assuming he was correct, I thought about his statement off and on during the day. If I can modify only one-tenth of my behavior, it doesn't provide incentive to make large, significant changes.

But perhaps that's good news for us. It means we need to focus on little things instead of a total makeover of our personality.

In fact, many experts say we can change, but we don't change much. Then I thought of a major, immediate transformation in my life and said aloud, "I quit smoking, and it was an abrupt decision." You see, I began to smoke when I was fifteen years old, which was about the age most of the kids in our neighborhood took up the habit. Six years later, and still smoking, I was in the US Navy stationed at Great Lakes, Illinois.

One evening, just before ten o'clock, I lay in my bunk, waiting for the noise in the barracks to stop and lights to go out so I could sleep. Eight hours earlier I had purchased a carton of cigarettes. Just then a shocking thought surfaced: *I don't need to smoke again.* And I knew with certainty those words were true. The decision was overpowering; I was convinced I wouldn't light up another cigarette.

I jumped out of my bunk and went to my locker. Pulling out the full carton and my lighter, I handed them to the man in the bunk next to me. "I quit. You can have them."

He laughed. "I'll give them back to you tomorrow."

"I don't want them back," I said. "I'm through for good."

He laughed again, but I meant what I said. I've never smoked since.

As I pondered that dramatic decision, I began a mental refutation of my pastor's message until I realized something: I had prepared for that powerful moment of transformation for eight months. I had taken tiny steps—mostly unsuccessful but serious attempts—toward quitting.

> I had prepared for that powerful moment of transformation for eight months.

For instance, I tried to limit myself to one cigarette every three hours; that decision lasted two days. I cut the cigarettes in half, which only made me want more. I smoked two packs of menthols to make me hate the taste, but that didn't eliminate my craving. I didn't know much about God in those days, but I prayed for help. I read an article in *Reader's Digest* about quitting smoking because of the health benefits, but the writer only advocated quitting without telling how.

Several friends gave me tips about how to give up smoking successfully, although none of them had done it. One of them insisted that I mix small amounts of tobacco with honey or jam and ingest it. That was supposed to guarantee I'd hate nicotine. It didn't work, although the experiment nauseated me. Chewing gum didn't provide a substitute. I chewed so much gum that I haven't desired to chew since.

I point out those many failures because they helped me make that dramatic shift in my behavior. I finally succeeded in accomplishing exactly what I had wanted to do for months. Those failures weren't true failures. To observers, my quitting appeared sudden and drastic, but I had been preparing my psyche for the shift.

Although I had tried a number of strategies, for eight months I didn't get the results I wanted. However, the trying helped me focus on what I wanted to accomplish. Instead of giving up (as many do), the failures pushed me to win over my addiction. *The small, unsuccessful steps kept me focused on what I wanted to accomplish.*

Of course, each time I fell short, I went through self-castigation and self-blame for failing again. But I moved beyond that by reminding myself that it had taken me at least a year before I became addicted; I probably needed that long to become un-addicted.

I refused to give up. Each time I started again with a new strategy. And isn't that the secret to making small attempts that lead to big success? We have to keep trying.

One failure doesn't count for much, but several failures at the same thing point out our seriousness to achieve. They remind us that we want to be different.

Instead of condemning ourselves for not making it, maybe it would help if we said, "Okay, I've learned one more way that won't work. I'll continue to try new approaches." Sometimes we only think we want to do something. The proof of wanting to make permanent change shows itself in persistence. The repeated attempts encourage us to know that we'll eventually achieve the results we want.

I won't focus on small failures.
I'll accept them as tiny steps toward big success.

8

Change Happens

ON TV I RECENTLY WATCHED part of an old 1940s film with Betty Grable called *The Shocking Miss Pilgrim.* The thin storyline, set at the end of the nineteenth century, was about Miss Pilgrim, the first female to work in an office. She was hired to be a typewriter (apparently that's what they called them in those days instead of typist.)

Much of the story centered around the resentment of the men toward having a woman in their office. They could have done more about their dislike of the actual typewriter machine, which would replace handwritten documents and throw some of them out of a job.

It was a light comedy, so I smiled. Then I thought of the advent of computers. The problems were similar. I bought my first computer—which we then called a *word processor*, because that's the only thing we used them to do—in 1983.

In the early 1980s, not many people were interested in learning about them or buying them.

"I do well with my electric typewriter," my secretary said. "And besides that, those things are so complicated." It was because of the hassle of inserting and ejecting huge floppy disks.

That was how it was in the beginning. And in those early days many of us typed faster than WordStar or WordPerfect software.

Ten years later a woman told me, "They said I had to learn to use one of those word-processing things, so I told them if I couldn't use my IBM Selectric, they could fire me."

She lost her job.

Since then, the issues have been different, but changes in every field affect the hiring and firing of personnel.

Many of us remember when e-mail came into being, and we struggled with addictions to the Internet cyber world. Many of us can talk about the time we bought our first cell phone as a portable telephone and nothing else.

There's one point I want to make: *Change. Change. Change. Life is changing and will continue to change.* We all know that, but I'm intrigued by the way it impacts us.

For some people, especially those who are the last ones to adapt, change threatens them. They won't say it, but they're afraid to learn something new, unlearn a way of doing things, or simply think differently.

I recently did my first webinar and began using Skype. I'm now blogging, and that took a lot of push from my assistant before I agreed. That's also called change.

Then there are the eager ones who see change as exciting and positive. Paul Price was the first one who talked to me about a word processor. He extolled their virtues and told me that typewriters would be obsolete in a decade. I don't know about the accuracy of his timeframe, but Paul was correct.

Paul epitomizes those who can see not only the immediate future but also around the bend in the road. They don't just see the obvious potential but glimpse what lies beyond that.

But what of those who want to lock themselves inside their office or chain themselves to the old workspaces? Even if they resist the change, it comes anyway.

We will accept most changes because they're inevitable. Take, for instance, bucket seats in cars, HD-TV, incandescent light bulbs, and cars with alternative fuels.

Those outward changes also push us to accept inward changes. We can't remain the same.

Changes will happen.
I can accept them now,
or I'll be forced to accept them later.

9

Small Steps, Bigger Goals

"I CAN CHANGE. I can be different."

I'll long remember the words the man cried out to his wife in my presence. The couple had come to me for help, even though I didn't consider myself a counselor. But I liked them, and both of them trusted me, which is why they asked me to help.

"I've had enough," she said quietly. "I don't have any more forgiveness in me." She went on to say she had forgiven him countless times for his mistreatment of her and their two daughters over the past nine years. And, to his credit, he didn't deny what he had done.

"But I can be different—"

"Oh, you change all right, but it's always temporary."

Their conversation went on for some time. Then he knelt before her with tears in his eyes and begged for "just one more chance."

"You've done this before—"

"But this time—"

She raised her hand to stop him. "Show me *permanent* transformation. In six months, if you can show me that you're really different, we can talk."

They left shortly after that. He kept his word—for nearly four months—before he went back to his abusive behavior. She filed for divorce.

I relate that story because he wanted things to be better. He wanted to be different. And he tried, but his efforts didn't last long. I think I know the reason: *he wanted to be different while he remained the same person.*

To permanently modify behavior for most of us means that we stop doing something or we give up long-held attitudes. That may include taking no action—being passive or inactive. But it takes more than a desire to be different.

- "I won't lose my temper again."
- "I won't spend money without consulting you."
- "I won't miss another day of work for the rest of the year."
- "I'll get things done exactly when I promise and not two days later."

To permanently modify behavior for most
of us means we stop doing something
or we give up long-held attitudes.

The intent to alter our behavior has to be as serious as the act of change. It needs to be more than a promise not to become angry or to decide to save money from each payday.

For any commitment to become permanent, it must begin on the inside, and it must be a choice. That doesn't make it easy, but it gives us a firm, inner foundation.

I remember when I quit smoking—back before it became the popular thing to do. As I said, I tried several methods, and none of them worked. One day I decided I had had enough. I had to take action that would stop one form of behavior and bring about a different result.

So I quit and never lit up again—and never desired to do so. Others have had similar experiences with smoking, weight loss, stopping sarcasm or gossip, or getting work done on time.

One reason so many good resolutions fail is that we try to alter too much at one time. It's like being in third grade and trying to read the massive novel *War and Peace*.

> For any commitment to become permanent, it must begin on the inside, and it must be a choice.

Instead, we usually win by implementing small, incremental steps. For example, I'm a high-energy, always-on-the-move person, and I used to work seven days a week. About a decade ago, I did research when I worked on a book about healthy living and longevity. In a study done by the National Institutes of Health and Loma Linda University, one of the key factors for longer and healthier living was that people rested one day every week. No work—total rest.[1]

That's been in the Judeo-Christian thinking from the beginning, but few of us seriously set aside the time. The more I researched, the more evidence I found that pointed to the fact that those who relaxed for twenty-four hours every seven days actually became more productive and experienced greater pleasure during the other six days.

I knew myself well enough to know that for me to cease anything productive one full day a week was impossible. But I believed I could do it by increments. I chose Sunday because we went to church that day anyway, and it meant I didn't do any work until the afternoon.

I deliberately chose to read for an hour after lunch. After two or three weeks, I increased that time to ninety minutes. Later I set aside two hours. It took me six months to be able to stop work for one day every week.

To my surprise, I produce as much as I did before, and Mondays have become different. Instead of groaning over what I didn't complete the day before, I'm ready to start the new week with fresh insight and renewed energy.

When we want to alter our life—and most of us have areas we need to modify—the best way is to make small, easy adaptations, get comfortable with them, and then move on to the next increment.

That method works for me—and I'm still learning. What I did may not work for everyone, but I'm convinced the principle is right.

To make change permanent,
I'll focus on small steps
that lead to a larger goal.

10

Rethinking Fitness

ONE OF THE BEST GIFTS I ever gave myself was to start a program of physical exercise. That decision changed my life in many ways. I've never been on a diet, but after six months of disciplined exercise, I lost the twenty-five-pound, basketball-sized lump around my waist. My blood pressure dipped.

More than exercising for the sake of exercising, I began it as a way to transform my lifestyle. I often walk to the library (almost a mile each way). Why not take the steps instead of the elevators? My rule inside a building is that if it's less than six flights, I walk. Or why not park at the far end of the shopping mall? Not only is there more space, but it provides an opportunity for a few hundred feet of physical exertion. One friend began riding his bicycle to do errands instead of driving. The idea is to build exercise into our lifestyles. With that approach, we can sustain physical movement for a longer time.

Sustain the activity—that's the point. The programs we start after overeating during the Christmas season don't work. Most gyms fill up in January with new memberships, and by February, a large number of those quick-fix zealots have dropped out. We give ourselves a variety of reasons we can't continue.

For some people, exercise seems a quick fix to lose weight or get in shape, but few people begin programs with the idea of sustaining them indefinitely.

So I'll tell you about myself. I began my exercising during a crisis time. Elsewhere I'll refer to "the white flight" and closing of our church; this was the right thing to do, but it brought me down emotionally. Even though I knew I had done the right thing, a number of the members criticized me—and some of it was extremely harsh and caused me a great deal of pain.

I had read that physical exercise is a wonderful way to alter our mood, so I decided to go that route. I joined a fitness center and did the heavy lifting (I never saw an increase in my pecs). I did the treadmill and swimming. I liked the swimming, but the treadmill became boring.

Finally, I began to run outside. That's when I formed a daily and lifelong exercise routine. I discovered I love to run, and it suits my temperament and my body type. It's not for everyone, but it works for me. Positive changes took place in my body. Best of all, my energy improved. I've always been energetic, but my exercise program enabled me to sustain that energy for a longer time.

The type of exercise isn't as important as the routine of doing it regularly. I began by running four days a week and walking three. I'm fortunate because I haven't had problems with knees or shin splints.

I go through all of this because the time when we most need to exercise is usually when we feel the least like it. When life is in confusion or we face disaster, the tendency is to feel enervated and lethargic and become a so-called couch potato. Crisis depletes us emotionally, spiritually, and intellectually. We may be angry or rage against injustice, but exercise seems to fall to the bottom of our to-do lists.

It takes quite an effort to get ourselves psyched up if we're not used to moving our bodies. But we can learn. I started by joining a friend at his health spa. I began my outside running by enlisting five other men. We ran every Saturday.

> The time when we most need to exercise is usually when we feel the least like it.

Even now, when I'm stuck on a writing project, I go for a run or a two-mile fast-paced walk. For me, something about moving my body frees me. Often I don't focus on the problem. In fact, I try to let my mind wander and think about anything else. At least that's how it starts.

My philosophy is that when my mindfulness (my conscious awareness) is at work, I feel stuck. When I think about other things, the unconscious part of me is free to work. When that part of me has the answer, it zooms to my awareness, and I'm ready to do something. My unconscious mind is at work while my conscious mind stares at the path ahead of me. By distracting myself from the problem, I actually move toward solving it.

Many mornings, near the end of my run, I'll face a question in my writing—not being sure what to do about a chapter or even one paragraph. Before I return home, however, I usually know the answer. Writing is what I do for a living, but I'm convinced this method works no matter our occupation or situation.

Sometimes the best way for us to get inner direction is not to seek it. To stop trying to solve the problem and allow God to whisper a solution. Because I don't like saying "God told me" and I'm rarely positive that's God speaking, I prefer to use terms such as my intuitive voice or inner wisdom.

Inner wisdom and *intuitive voice* may not be accurate terms, but that's how I explain it to myself. In any situation, when I don't know what to do or my world has gone chaotic, I know there are solutions for me. It may be doing something small, such as making a phone call, texting, or sending an e-mail. Or the answer may be to wait and relax.

The discipline of an exercise program is one of the wisest things I do for myself. When I began, I didn't know how I could find half an hour to run. Now I run for about an hour and don't know how I could live without hoofing it.

Another point is that we need to find the best time for our exercise program. My friend David likes to walk with his dog around two thirty in the morning—before he goes to bed. I like to wake up around four thirty and start my day with a five-mile run. It's a matter of finding our own rhythm and discovering what physical movement we like best, as well as the right time—the time that fits our schedule.

Experts talk about the release of endorphins during exercise. I haven't made a study of it myself. Perhaps that's what happens. But this much I know about the results of a serious exercise routine: I'm always calmer and more at peace afterward.

I exercise regularly—
but I do it for more than physical results.

11

Letting It Go

"OH, IT'S JUST A NEW JOB," Josh told me. "You know, I'll do the same thing as I did before, but I'll make more money and have a shorter commute."

I smiled and wondered if it would be "just" a new job. The tendency for most of us is to minimize events when we decide to make changes, especially those that we don't ponder for a long time. The opportunity seems good, we think about it, and finally make the move. If we decide to initiate change (instead of it being forced on us, such as the loss of a job or a death), we tend to minimize the importance of endings.

"You'll have adjustments," I said to Josh.

"Minor stuff."

"Make sure you've let go of your old job," I said.

Josh is a man who connects well with people. I had a feeling he had left the building, but he hadn't taken all of himself into his new position.

Josh stared at me, shrugged, started to walk away...and said, "If I make the ending of my old job significant, it means I've made a mistake—"

He didn't give me the opportunity to respond, but I understood what he meant. He wanted to focus on the positive and forget every negative factor of the past.

If only it were that easy.

Josh thought that being concerned would suggest he had made a mistake in changing jobs. Or it might mean that he should have done something different. I knew that in time the past would catch up with him and he'd have to rethink what he had done. He'd have to face a letting-go period.

No matter how good the present becomes because of change, we need to release the hold of the old ways. We have to hit the release button to move forward. As long as we compare the present situation with the previous one, we haven't let go.

"I like my job and it's good, but the pressure is stronger," Josh said a month after he switched companies. "My boss can be short-tempered, and my previous boss was so easy to get along with."

Josh didn't say he'd made a mistake, but he was still holding on to *what had been* and couldn't fully appreciate *what is*. He compared the old with the new.

I mention this because letting go is vital to grabbing hold. When we're forced to change, the situation is worse and we often find it difficult to admit that the life we're moving into could be as good or even better. If we don't let go, we can't grasp the good in the change.

Modifying or adapting is strange and often confusing. "One does not discover new lands without consenting to lose sight of the shore for a very long time" is a quote attributed to André Gide. And that's how it works.

> Letting go
> is vital to
> grabbing hold.

Change isn't always easy—even if it's something we've wanted and dreamed of for years. Most of us tend to minimize the ending.

- "I wasn't treated fairly."
- "I worked harder than the others in my division."
- "It was a mistake to stay as long as I did."
- "I should have done something differently in preparing to quit."

If change was forced—a company relocates and leaves us behind or eliminates our position through downsizing—often nothing seems good about the situation.

Our natural tendency is to forget the past job or the past relationships. We jump into the new role or seek new friends or lovers and shut off the past. "I don't want to think about that," we say. "I'm glad it's over."

But it's not over for most of us. We remember the things that led up to adjusting our life. We may have initiated the alteration, or it may have been forced on us. Either way, I want to suggest we pause and reflect on those past experiences.

Our major task in making a different career, taking a new path, or adjusting without a loved one is to release the past. We don't have to forget what was. Instead we need to remember that this is now, and this is the way our life is—what some call "the new normal." The past may have been wonderful and blissful. But that's not where we live now.

To appreciate what I have now,
I need to separate myself from what was before.

12

Feeling Disenchanted?

DISENCHANTMENT IS PART OF THE TRANSITION from the old to the new. We look at ourselves, examine our lives, and feel as if where we are now is largely due to self-deception.

- *I thought I knew who I was, but I was wrong.*
- *I was sure this was the dream job, but I was badly misled.*
- *I'm making more money, but I'm enjoying my life much less.*
- *Isn't there something more in life than this?*

One question that comes up hits the core of our being: *If I'm not who I thought I was, who am I?*

Thirty years ago my friend Tom was the pastor of a conservative congregation. Most of the members were appalled at the concept of divorce—especially among clergy. Tom decided to divorce his wife of more than twenty years (the reasons aren't important for the topic of this chapter). He felt it was the right thing to do, but he faced serious consequences. He assumed the members of the congregation would demand that he resign.

"Even if they do," he said, "I can't tolerate the marriage any longer."

He had trained to be a minister and hadn't seriously considered any other career path. "It's who I am," he said to me. "And if I'm not a minister, who am I?"

> "If I'm not who I thought I was, who am I?"

I didn't know the answer, so I said nothing.

"Has my life been one of lying to myself? Have I deceived myself into thinking I am someone I'm not?"

The questions went on and on as we strolled along the sands beside the Atlantic Ocean.

For at least half an hour Tom asked the same questions—different words but the same issues. He had become disenchanted with life. He was sure he was a fraud and certain everyone would know he couldn't live up to the life he professed.

I've met others who've gone through similar disenchantment. Sometimes they refer to it as *burnout*. "It's time to make a change," they might say. They talk about their high ideals and strong goals when they started a job or a task. They were sure they would succeed. And sometimes they did. Yet sometimes success wasn't the answer, and instead, they asked a question.

"Is this all there is?"

I've been at that place. I was the pastor of a metropolitan church. For the first six years I thought I could stay there for the rest of my professional career. And I meant it. I felt I had the best situation possible—as the pastor of a growing church, a writer who was selling books and articles, and an adjunct professor at a local college.

> "Is this all there is?"

About the middle of the eighth year, disenchantment—or *restlessness*—tapped me on the shoulder. I tried new programs and various kinds of outreach to the community. We became known as a congregation of caring people. When community organizations needed help, we were the first ones they called, and the members supported those things. I won the respect of my peers and people in the community.

"Is this really what I want to do?"

I recognized those things, but the doubts grew. "Is this really what I want to do?" I felt as if I had become mechanical in many of the things I did. I questioned whether I was as effective as I could be. And the disenchantment progressed.

Although I was unable to grasp what was going on, my restlessness opened the door for me to move into something else. I didn't like the way my life was unfolding. I would have preferred an abrupt awareness and to be able to say, "I liked what I did. Now I have a new quest. I'm ready to move on."

But I didn't move on.

The restlessness increased. I became irritable over small things and chided myself for my lack of enthusiasm. No one else seemed to notice the difference, but I was aware.

For me, it took more than a year to make a drastic change. I often asked myself, *What's wrong? I loved what I was doing, so why don't I feel the same way now?*

Only in retrospect did I figure out a significant principle in the messiness of life: disenchantment is a necessary condition before we're ready to change.

Until disenchantment sets in, I'm not ready to make changes.

13

The Importance of the Search

"I WISH I KNEW WHAT TO DO," my friend said after we had talked for nearly thirty minutes. "I'm tired of not knowing what lies ahead. I'm wearied by being uncertain. I pray for clarity, but none comes."

I sensed that no matter what I said, it wouldn't have mattered. My friend had to work out his own issues, and I couldn't solve his problem for him.

After our conversation, I replayed many of his words. At first I felt sorry for him because I knew the turmoil and confusion he had been enduring for at least a month. It was sad to see a normally happy person walking around dejected and depressed.

Just then a series of questions popped into my mind.

- What if the searching is as important as the finding?
- What if he *needs* to go through this dark time?
- What if the uncertainty makes the future even more wonderful because of what he must endure to get there?

As I pondered, I realized that we don't like uncertainty. We like things laid out for us. We can't figure out why, just when our world seems stable and we are experiencing our best moments, we trip over some unforeseen bump. Disorientation takes place.

- "I don't get it."
- "I don't understand."
- "I hate this confusion."

- "What did I do wrong?"
- "Do I deserve this?"

We don't like uncertainty. We like things laid out for us.

I've said those very words in the midst of the messes of life. Many times I've thought that I could take the worst possible news as long as I knew what was happening. *Not knowing* is the place of angst and frustration.

But my friend's problem sent my thinking in a new direction.

- What if searching and confusion are the ways we gain insight into our lives?
- What if we *need* the quest and the seeking to discover new paths?
- What if those "bad times" are the only paths we have to take us into the better times?
- What if the bad times are really the good times, but we won't figure that out until later?

I also wondered if searching and walking in dark places were worse than following the same path day after day and never venturing into something new.

The day after my friend opened up, we talked again for a long time. Much of it was recycling his complaints and anger at his messy life.

Finally he said, "I hate these constant changes in my life. I want stability."

"Are you sure?"

"You think this is fun?"

"No, I don't, but consider this. The things you want to hold on to and the changes you want to prevent are the very things that came about by previous changes in your life. And you fought some of them too."

He started to object, so I repeated the words. I've known him for nine years, and I reminded him of some of the positive changes he had experienced in his personal life, his business world, and even the church he attended.

"I guess I had forgotten," he said.

"The search—the journey, or whatever you want to call it—may be more significant than the result. Maybe you need the anxiety to make you ready to embrace the new."

He smiled and thanked me.

"When I go through the next time of anxiety in my life," I said, "I hope I can count on you to remind me of what I've just said to you. I don't like going through change, but I generally like the results." Those words took me back to where I had started ruminating about my friend.

The searching isn't as important as the finding:
it's more important.

14

Who's Got Your Back?

WHEN I WROTE A BOOK WITH MATT LOEHR called *Who's Got Your Back? Why We Need Accountability*, I did it because I believed in the principles Matt wanted to stress. The essence of the book is that all of us need someone to guard our back—or to back us up.

Some speak of them as *accountability partners*, and I like that term. If done right, it means we have someone to whom we can open ourselves and who seeks to understand us.

I have such a person in David Morgan. Until I began to work with Matt, Dave and I called ourselves *friends*. But using Matt's definition, we've been *accountability partners* for thirty years.

Our special relationship began with a simple realization. Neither of us remembers who said it, so I'll take credit. I said to David, "You've been everybody's best friend, but you never *had* a best friend."

As we talked, both of us decided we wanted a best friend, and we moved gradually into becoming just that.

We meet together weekly (when possible) for one or two hours and talk about what's going on inside us. Our attempt is to open ourselves to each other as fully as possible. Our trust and affection built up slowly. David once said my "irrefutable love" enabled him to open himself to me.

Because of that experience and a few others, I'm a strong advocate of building accountability relationships. Here are the three factors that make this important to me.

First, *I speak freely to my accountability partner about the things inside me.* Because of who he is, David has never laughed at me when I've told him things about myself. His acceptance encourages me to "own" my words. Until I share them verbally with another person, they may be important or highly significant, but I don't declare ownership until I speak them.

For example, years ago I said to Joan Wheatley, a good friend to Shirley and me, "I want to write books."

I started to laugh as if I were kidding, but she said, "Why not? I think you could do that."

When I began to write, her affirming my intention was a powerful motivator. I had declared myself and my desires. Now it was no longer a secret or hidden deeply inside my heart.

Accountability Partner:
Someone to whom we can open ourselves
and who seeks to understand us.

The second important factor in an accountability relationship is that *I declare a course of action and my accountability partner reminds me.* The reminding may be as strong as rebuking or as gentle as nudging, but it means I will take action or say, "I can't do it."

Third, *my accountability partner acts as a "reality check."* Sometimes I think I see things clearly, and David gently nudges me by commenting, "Here's another way to interpret that..." Without pushing or insisting, he tells me his perception. He's usually correct.

Sometimes I rebut his words by asking, "Aren't you talking more about yourself than you are about me?" Because of our long-standing friendship, we can talk that way.

Above all, I know David "has my back." I'm not fully comfortable with that phrase; I prefer to think of it as David loving me (as I love him) and wanting only the best of everything for me.

When life doesn't make sense, when I'm caught up in a situation and too emotional to think clearly, I easily misconstrue words or meanings. Because my accountability partner is able to be objective about my situation, he can help me get the right perspective on life.

*Having the help of an accountability partner
means having someone make sense
for me when life doesn't.*

15

Facing Rejections

"Don't take this personally," my friend said.

I stared at him and wondered how I could not take the rebuff personally. It had happened *to me*. It seemed easy enough for him to talk like that because my crisis didn't affect him. I was bleeding emotionally, and he was telling me how *not* to feel.

I had been rejected. It wasn't the first time in my life, but that fact didn't make it easier to accept. And it's probably true with most of us. Rejections aren't new to any of us. We experienced them the day Mom took our favorite toy and gave it to our sibling, when we were the last one chosen on the playground, and when we applied for a job and the human resources person smirked at our résumé.

I'm a specialist in rejection because I'm a professional writer. Part of the job description includes learning to accept rejections—many rejections—and most of us never get beyond that. That's true with anyone in sales, and in one sense, I'm in sales.

For any of us who sell books, real estate, clothes, or insurance policies, the principle applies. None of us wins every time. Sometimes the customer says no. Or we don't get the promotion we're convinced we're owed. Or we hear the buzzword *downsize,* and it means, "I'm out of a job."

How can I not take that personally?

I've read dozens of articles and books and heard many lectures about rejections, but they haven't helped a great deal. When someone says no to me and it's something I want, it *is* personal.

As a writer, I came to terms with the despised word by telling myself jokingly that I was selling a product (my book manuscript), and the editor wasn't bright enough to sense the value of my pristine prose. That helped me objectify the situation.

> When someone says no to me and it's something I want, it *is* personal.

Even so, it took me a long, long time to be able to depersonalize a refusal. Part of that was because I was trying to make a good living from my craft, and to receive a non-acceptance was like a major detour off the highway I wanted to follow.

It is personal. What happens when the rejection is something that affects your livelihood? What happens when you need a loan and the bank says, "Sorry, you're not qualified"? Or how do you take it objectively when your spouse, whom you love, wants to leave?

I don't know the answer to those situations, but I can share my insights in dealing with them.

It's all right to wallow in pain, hurt, anger, depression, or any other emotion you feel. It's all right—*for a while.*

What's wrong with feeling those things that hurt us? Real living means being honest about ourselves.

In the middle of the pain, talk to a few friends—the right friends. Find a shoulder or two on which to rest your head. A hug. A word of encouragement and empathy.

The time comes when we need to move beyond self-pity (and that's what it really is). We've admitted we failed or didn't get what we wanted. Now what do we do?

I can respond in two ways.

First, *because of my faith in God, I realize I've been in situations as bad or worse, and my faith has pulled me through.* I made it in the past, I can make it in the present.

> Real living means being honest about ourselves.

When my life doesn't make sense, I have one statement that I say to myself, and it works: "Who am I to think that I should be immune?"

Some people seem to think that if we believe in God, that separates us from others who have misfortune. Or they assume that if we're morally upright, we won't face injustice.

I don't agree with that attitude. My faith is in a God who doesn't shield me from chaos but who is with me during the chaos.

Second, *I can turn to my experience.* If I survived rejections of the past—and I have—I can survive this.

In the past it may have started with not getting the part in a play or losing an election for class president. In our teen years, the one person we wanted to date turned us down—perhaps even laughed at us—but we survived. We can do the same now.

Surviving rejections and failed plans in the past assures me that I can handle them in the present.

16

Paving the Way

DURING THE PERIOD OF "THE WHITE FLIGHT," I was an inner-city pastor. When church members talked about what to do, they affirmed they would stay and integrate schools, neighborhoods, and churches. I think they meant the words they spoke, but they were unable to fulfill their promises. Most of them moved within a three-year period.

During that time, I learned to figure out when people were going to move out of the community long before they said anything. I'm not sure they were aware before I was.

The first sign was a complaint or a note of discontent. "Have you noticed how the black people...?" Sometimes they didn't make an ethnic statement, but their voices implied one. Their comments varied, but all of them came down to two things: the new people in the community didn't have the same values they did, and they themselves weren't willing to adjust to the new people.

Once the members voiced their complaints, it usually took two or three more months before a FOR SALE sign went up in their yards.

I mention that ancient history to point out that we usually pave the way for change by the things we think or say. The new direction is already set long before we take action. Things have often been at work within us long before we become aware of them.

For example:

- We lose enthusiasm for our work.
- We become critical of coworkers or our neighborhoods.
- We keep silent about our spouse's infidelity for ten years, then begin to speak about his terrible ways.

We show our discontent by saying things such as:

- "I used to love working for my company and felt I would stay there for the rest of my working life. But they let me down."
- "They keep adding responsibility to my job and don't give me more money."
- "My spouse betrayed me, and I just couldn't live with it anymore."

As I wrote the words above, I thought of something my friend Dr. David Morgan said years ago. He taught a course for professionals on how to help people cope with divorce. One of the first things he said was that, in his experience, it usually took about two years from the time individuals began to think about divorce until they took any action. (I assume, like everything else, the process is faster these days.)

> We usually pave the way for change by the things we think or say.

In short, something happens that disrupts our lives or makes us resentful, and we want to change, but we're not ready. We may not even be ready to face the reality. Our expressed thoughts may be our way to slowly tell ourselves, *I want things to be different.*

We're probably not even aware of anything happening—at least nothing specific or concrete—yet that unconscious part of ourselves may be making inward preparation for weeks or months before we realize that we want to do something differently.

Again, I refer to my years as a pastor. I liked being a pastor. Most days I was out of bed within seconds of awakening. I could hardly wait to get out of the house and do the things I had scheduled. For twelve of my fourteen years I continued to feel that way. But something began to happen to me in the middle of that twelfth year. You might call it *burnout* or *dissatisfaction*, but there was nothing negative to which I could point. We were still a vibrant, growing congregation.

But one day—about the end of year thirteen—I began to ask myself, *Is this what I really want to do?*

Sometimes I'd ask, *I still have a lot of years left in the work force. Is this where I want to stay until I retire?*

A number of opportunities came for me to move to larger churches, but that didn't appeal to me. "Five hundred people are about as many as I can wrap my arms around," I said. "And I have that many now."

I realized I had lost a little enthusiasm for new projects. A few times I heard myself ask, *Do I make a difference?*

They were good questions...all quiet and inner nudges that pushed Shirley and me closer to the awareness that something had to change. And even more than that "something," we finally faced what we needed to do.

When that "something" comes to the level of awareness, we're ready to take action. But too many want to push forward, to truncate the time and move more quickly .

When we're ready, we intuitively seem to know. That's the right time to make a change.

I choose to go a different direction when I'm ready. And when I'm ready, something inside whispers, "Now is the time."

17

The Path Behind Us

YEARS AGO I READ SOMETHING that sounds similar to this statement: Change is the path ahead; change is also the path behind.

I had to think about those statements for quite a while, especially the path behind. Then I figured it out. We come to the crossroads of life—we all do in a multitude of ways. Sometimes those decision points are extremely dramatic, such as which job to take, which person to date, where to live, or what organization to join.

We fill our lives with other times when we deviate from where we're headed. They're often small decisions, which at the time seem insignificant but often have long-term effects. Because they're small, we pay little attention to them and don't realize that we are changing.

I point this out because I frequently hear people complain that things aren't the way they used to be. Of course they aren't! Life isn't static, even for those who do mechanical, routine jobs for eight hours a day.

I also think many of those memories are faulty. They recall the good of the past and forget the angst and pain of those days. Regardless, each day we make decisions.

When I wrote *90 Minutes in Heaven* with Don Piper, we made it clear that the accident that killed Don shot him to heaven. Later, he returned to earth. That entire event happened because Don made a choice that, on the surface, seemed insignificant.

Don had attended a conference and decided on an alternate road from the retreat setting to Houston.

"There were two ways to get back to Houston.... I had to choose either to drive through Livingston and down Highway 59 or to head west to Huntsville and hit I-45, often called the Gulf Freeway.... Either choice is probably about the same distance.... That morning I decided to take the Gulf Freeway."[2]

That simple turn of the wheel altered the course of his future. The story is extremely dramatic, but the principle applies to each of us every day. We often speak of coincidences, accidents, freakish timing, or unexpected events, but most of the time we alter our world by a combination of little things we did in the past.

Right now life may not make sense. We might even ask ourselves, *How did I get into this mess?* Or we might wonder, *What did I do to get so lucky?* We can't see the future, but our past attitudes and actions set us up for the future. A big reason we're where we are now is because we chose—wisely or unwisely. Sometimes we don't even realize we're making decisions.

> We alter our world by a combination of little things we did in the past.

Years ago, Betty Stewart told me she twisted her foot at the curb. She wasn't hurt, but the heel of her pump came off. While she wondered what to do, she looked around. Two doors up on her left was a shoe repair store. She'd passed that way for more than a year and never noticed it before.

She went inside. While she waited for the man to repair her shoe, a young man walked in to have his shoes resoled. He recognized her as someone who worked in his building. They began to chat.

Six months later Betty married the man. A little thing like losing the heel on a shoe changed her life.

We constantly face risks and adventures. But more often it's the seemingly insignificant choices that strongly determine our future. Although it's too long a story to share here, I'm a serious Christian today simply because I paused in front of a bookstore in Waukegan, Illinois, and stared at a used book that grabbed my attention. I bought the book, and that pushed me to read the Bible, which started an agnostic sailor on a spiritual quest. I hadn't been inside a church since I was eleven years old.

Small decisions often produce dramatic results. Much of what lies behind me prepares me for what lies ahead.

18

Becoming Resilient

WHEN I WAS FORTY-FOUR, my father died of a stroke. On the day of his funeral, my older brother died of cancer. I knew Ray was sick, but I wasn't aware of how close to death he was.

The six of us surviving siblings were at the family home and one of my sisters asked, "Who's going to tell Mom?" My mother was one of those people who cried over almost anything, so it was a significant ordeal for us.

"How do you think she lived to be this old?" I asked. "She's handled things like this before."

"Then you tell her," my sister Evelyn said.

That wasn't what I meant, but I agreed to talk to Mom. I called her aside and told her about Ray. She nodded, left me, and went into her bedroom. Perhaps thirty minutes later, she came out and seemed quite normal.

As I stared at her, I understood. Mom was resilient. She had the ability to face the horror of two deaths—her husband of more than sixty years and the death of her fifty-three-year-old firstborn son.

Resilience. That's the ability to bounce back, to accept the worst news, and to keep going.

At the time I didn't think of myself as *resilient*—a word I reserved for those who faced the most catastrophic conditions and survived. Those tough, rugged people who lived through earthquakes, bombings, and faced death, yet didn't seem overwhelmed.

That day, as I watched my mother, I grasped that she had the toughness of resilience—the ability to accept what can't be changed and not be defeated by it. It's an inner strength.

And how do we develop that fortitude? By living each day and pulling ourselves up after each seeming defeat.

Resilience—the ability to accept what can't be changed and not be defeated by it.

My mother had become a strong Christian, and certainly her faith enabled her to hold up. And I believe that's when faith becomes most important—when life falls apart. Some go through a painful divorce, or the deception by someone previously considered a friend. Perhaps a request for a loan to buy a house gets turned down. Or a car dies on you, or you're involved in a serious accident.

That's when faith makes sense. That's when we realize we need help and call on a power beyond our own abilities. If we call out and trust God's loving care through our hard times, we survive and build resilience.

The most resilient person with whom I've ever worked is Don Piper. Most people know of the book we did together, *90 Minutes in*

Heaven. After Don returned to earth, he endured thirty-four surgeries. He lives in pain every day. He can't bend like most people. I could go on down the list of his physical traumas. None of them slow him down.

Our book came off the press in the fall of 2004. Since then, Don has averaged more than two hundred speaking engagements each year. And yes, sometimes he is exhausted, and he's had to cancel a few times because he's worn out. But three or four days later, he's back on the road. That's a toughness I don't observe in many people.

Don and my mother make a principle obvious to me. Most of us pray for and yearn for life to be easy—and I'm no exception. I hate setbacks and hardships. If we survive disappointments—and we do—each survival strengthens us for the next one, which will probably be a little bigger.

That's resilience—the ability to fall into the deepest holes, dig our way out, and keep dancing down the unclear path ahead. Sure, we'll fall again. But we've learned to crawl, creep, walk, or run because we refuse to give up. In the learning process, we've become more pliable and flexible.

Life doesn't always make sense, and we have no explanations for the disappointments or setbacks, yet we can become tougher and stronger than we were before the confusion invaded our world.

If I live through hardships,
resilience is the payoff.

19

Understanding Pain

MOST OF US TRY to make sense of our pain, heartaches, and losses. In my opinion, no one has done that better than Holocaust survivor Viktor Frankl in his 1946 book, *Man's Search for Meaning.* Still in print, the book touches many people because Frankl described the inhumanity and the suffering around him. But even more than that, he grappled with the insanity of the Nazi regime. Even though people around him died every day, he found meaning and purpose.

When the prisoners in the concentration camp had hope—something to dream about and think about, such as being reunited with a loved one—they survived the most excruciating punishments. When they learned that their wives or children were dead, however, they fell into despair and died shortly afterward.

Frankl made sense out of pain and human suffering by looking beyond it to better times ahead. Most of us want to make sense of what goes on around us, but we can't understand some things, such as emotional pain, injustice, or ruthless loss of life.

The worst is when the messiness of life takes place and we can't make sense out of our situations. We're confused because we've tried to live by certain principles and remain true to what we believe, yet chaos still envelops us. We think:

- *If I work hard, my employer will appreciate me, and I'll always have a job.*
- *If I remain faithful to those I love, we'll live together in happiness and tranquility.*
- *If I take care of myself, I'll live a long and healthy life. I'll ward off sickness.*
- *If I'm a good person, and I treat people fairly, I'll have a good life.*
- *I'm a serious believer in God, so I'll live a happy, blessed life.*

But sometimes disappointments and setbacks come anyway. Life surprises us—beats us up and confuses us. We think we've figured out the way to navigate through problems so we can drive freely down the road of contentment. That's when we hit another IB—inevitable bump—those unexpected and usually unwanted shifts or challenges that force us to take a different path. However, heartaches, disappointments, betrayal, all forms of pain, never stop.

How do we respond? Do we stop trying to figure out those things or quit working through the anguish? Probably not; we can learn to grow through the process.

We think we've figured out the way to navigate through problems so we can drive freely down the road of contentment. That's when we hit another IB—inevitable bump.

That's the good thing to say about understanding suffering and hardship. In the process we don't usually receive startling self-revelations, have moments of spiritual enlightenment, or figure out why calamities strike us. Instead, we persevere even when we don't have the slightest idea how or why such things happen. In the process we grow stronger by facing the turmoil. And once we become stronger through getting up and continuing to struggle, understanding begins to filter through.

I can't explain the reasons some have more heartaches and roadblocks than others or why others seem (at least outwardly) to coast along with few problems.

I've finally learned to stop trying to make sense out of things beyond my control. Life *is* messy and confusing. Some things didn't make sense in the past, and they don't thirty years later.

For me, it's enough to know I don't have to focus on all the distress and sadness. Like Frankl and others, I realize there's more to life than figuring it out.

I say to myself regularly, "This is what is." I don't have to understand or to make sense of it. I can choose to live it.

Recently I read these words by an unknown author, and they resonate with me: "Suffering colors all of my life, but I can choose the color."

I don't understand pain;
I don't understand suffering.
But I'm alive, and my life has meaning.

20

It Feels Like Death

"IT FELT LIKE DEATH, AND IT WAS," she said, and her eyes moistened. "After fourteen years, our marriage died—even though I now realize that it had been terminally ill for at least two years."

She told me she had cried, pleaded, and presented every argument possible to prevent his leaving her. As with any other traumatic experience, she felt separated from her old life and alienated from the things she had come to value.

"I seemed to have nothing to hold on to and no one who cared," she said. "That wasn't true, but that's how I felt."

She went on to say that she thought of his leaving her as the "death rattle" and the final termination came with the divorce papers. "As long as I looked back and hoped we'd find a way to work things out or that he'd beg me to forgive him," she said, "I was denying the finality of the situation."

After a few weeks of numbness and emotional dearth, she said to herself, *It's time to live again. I was dead, but now I'm alive.* Once she made up her mind and engaged herself once again in life, she was able to integrate change.

I mentally applauded my friend. She didn't want to lose her husband of fourteen years, but once it became a reality, she accepted it and took the next step. She was determined to move forward with her life. That was a drastic step of courage.

We talked a long time and near the end of our conversation she asked, "Why did it take so long for me to accept the death of the marriage? In all honesty, I knew it was inevitable years before it happened—"

"But you weren't ready to face it, were you?" I asked.

She stared into space a long time before she said, "I didn't want to face the truth. To do that meant I had made a mistake—many mistakes." She said it would have been easy to blame him and tell her friends what a rotten person he was. "But I didn't do that. I faced the reality that both of us had contributed to the death of our marriage."

"Everything in this world dies," one of my cynical friends said.

And he is right. Death is a big factor in living. Besides the death of a marriage or the physical death of loved ones, there is the end of a job by retirement, downsizing, or the inability to keep up with innovation. Once we realize that loss is part of life, it can help us enjoy people and relationships more while we have them.

My friend Barry Spencer knew his father was dying. Although Barry lived in another state, he flew home at least twice a month to spend days at a time with his father. They talked, and Barry asked his father countless questions. "I really wanted to know my dad," he told me.

His father's impending death made Barry realize he wanted their last days together to be meaningful. If it hadn't been for the warning signs of death, such as heart attack, bypass surgery, and heart transplant, he wouldn't have been so concerned to know his father.

Death comes in many forms, but it's also part of life.

The more I understand about death,
the more I embrace life.

21

The Right People Come Through

"I LOST MY JOB and found my real passion in life," the man said in front of the TV camera. "Now I'm happier than I've ever been."

Three others followed and told of being depressed and worried until they became what they'd always wanted to be. All of them had started small businesses that succeeded.

As I listened, I wondered about the people who aren't entrepreneurs and don't have some deeply hidden passion to open a store that sells only marvelous cupcakes and quiches. What about those people who simply want to work so they can bring in money and enjoy their lives?

Another segment of the program told about those who became volunteers while they waited for job opportunities. Great idea, but that's not for everyone either.

When good people who work faithfully at their jobs find themselves without the ability to buy food, pay utilities, and handle mortgage payments out of their meager savings and unemployment benefits, what can they do?

I don't know.

Each of us has to figure that out.

I was caught once in that unemployment squeeze and didn't know what to do myself. I had been the pastor of a church in the middle of an ethnically changing neighborhood. Members of the church couldn't open their arms and hearts to the newcomers, and many of them found reasons to move from the community.

I pushed the church elders to make a decision. "We paint, or we get off the ladder. If we get off the ladder, we give someone else the paintbrushes."

After six months, they agreed with me. We turned the facilities over to an African-American congregation, and we dispersed. That left me unemployed. They kindly voted to pay me my salary for one year, but I still had no position.

I had a part-time job with our denomination that took about two hours a week, but it was a make-work role for me. Aside from doing all the usual things of trying to get a new job, I went the route of self-examination.

Right then my life didn't make sense. I hated the situation I was in, even though the church had done the right thing for me.

I didn't get much support from friends and colleagues. I did hear lectures and clichéd words of encouragement. Many of the people I'd expected to be supportive disappeared from my life. The boosts came from the unexpected—people I scarcely knew.

For example, a former classmate, a man I had spoken to perhaps three times during our college years, mailed me an encouraging note every week for one year.

Another time, just as I reached the door of a university library, a professor whom I knew only by sight called my name. He shook my hand and said, "I've heard about your situation and I want you to know I care."

I was skeptical until he wrote his phone number on a piece of paper and stuck it in my shirt pocket. "If you don't call me, I'll call you."

Two weeks later he called. After that, every Friday morning I received a phone call from him for several months.

Many of the people I'd expected to be supportive disappeared from my life. The boosts came from the unexpected— people I scarcely knew.

Those unexpected acts of kindness from unexpected individuals came often enough to encourage me. And yet, despite their boost, my situation didn't make sense. I had done what I considered the honorable thing by pushing our church to close. I'm still convinced it was the correct decision. What I didn't grasp was the internal stress I would have to go through. Five months into my "new normal," I lay in a hospital bed for two days with an ulcer.

That's an example of trying to make sense when life doesn't. I did learn from my experience (despite the ulcer). I was forced to assess my life. One of the questions I asked daily was, "Is this what I want to do with the rest of my life?"

I had started on a career path, and I had to decide if I wanted to veer from it. Because prayer is an important part of my life, I prayed fervently and often each day. I didn't hear God speak or receive any miracle, but I grew.

In less than a year I received the call to become pastor of a church where I stayed—and happily—for a decade until I left to write full-time.

But I didn't know I would have a happy ending. I didn't know what lay ahead. I did know I would survive, and a few special people, including my wife, my former classmate, and a professor, were there for me to lean on. That, in itself, was a powerful lesson. I was forced to reach out to others because I couldn't handle the emotional pain alone.

And the right people came through.

The right people—the people we need at that moment—always come through.

I can't choose my circumstances;
I can't choose those who will support me.
But I can appreciate people who
care for me in my pain.

22

Our Hurting Friends

THE WORST TIME in my professional life happened during "the white flight" period I've previously mentioned. I became pastor of a fairly affluent congregation when leaders insisted I was the only one who could do it because

- "You lived in Africa." ("The Africans aren't the same as American blacks," I protested, but they didn't listen.)
- "You handled the integration well in your previous congregation." (True, but they were poor whites or elderly and unable to move.)
- "You're innovative and creative." (The flattering words seduced me.)

By the end of the second year at the new church, I was discouraged and wondered what I was doing on a white island in the middle of a black sea.

One day I confided in Joe, another pastor. His church, by contrast, flourished. Many of the white-flighters joined his congregation, which was only five miles from us, but that wasn't his fault or mine.

We stood outside my garage one day when I was at my lowest point.

To his credit, Joe listened to my complaints and confusion. Until that experience, in whatever I'd tried, I had been successful. I had confidence in my ability, and few doubts about what I could do. After I visited the African Americans in our community, one black family joined our church and three other children came regularly to Sunday school. Meanwhile, the Caucasian membership slowly declined. Several members informed me that if more blacks came, they would leave.

There was no way for me to win. And I told all that to Joe.

When I finally stopped talking, Joe put his hand on my right shoulder. I could see the compassion in his eyes. "After this is all over, one day you'll be able to look back and see it as a powerful time of growth."

I nodded, but I thought, *Don't you think I know that? But I don't care about the future or even next month. I hurt now. Right now!*

The platitudes began and Joe went on for the next twenty minutes. He must have quoted a dozen Bible verses. I couldn't argue with a single thing he said, but it wasn't at all helpful.

I still hurt.

I didn't need preaching, and I didn't need assurance that God was with me or that I'd come out stronger and more mature later.

I wanted relief. I wanted someone to care.

Joe meant well, and he thought he was encouraging me. Or maybe something else was going on. Maybe Joe was thinking of himself and what would happen when the white flight hit his church. (And it did three years later.) Joe moved to Texas just about the time it started.

Of course he was right about everything he said. My life did get better, and I grew as a direct result of the stress in those days. But Joe didn't help me when I needed him.

> *I still hurt. I wanted relief. I wanted someone to care.*

Maybe that's how it works with a lot of us. People face hardships and want our compassion and assistance. We give them words—and too often they're empty words. They're probably true, but inappropriate.

Did I care that *one day* I'd look back at that as a time of strong spiritual and inner growth? Absolutely not! I just wanted to emotionally survive that day.

Months ago I witnessed a similar situation. Jeff asked four of us to meet with him for lunch. After we'd eaten, he opened up. He was fifty years old, had lost his job, and despite sending out résumés and contacting people he hoped would help, nothing happened.

"My severance package comes to an end tomorrow. My wife's income barely pays the mortgage. I don't know what to do."

I knew what was coming, and I wasn't mistaken. Jeff got hit from three fronts with essentially the same message: "You'll survive, and you'll be stronger after this is over."

I said nothing—not because I was so wise but because I had been where Jeff was. I sat quietly, my head down, trying to figure out some word of comfort or encouragement.

One of the men pulled out his iPad, because he had downloaded the entire Bible. He read passages to Jeff. He had a good selection of wonderful words of hope and encouragement.

After perhaps twenty minutes, Jeff did something I wish I had done when I was faced with the advice givers. He slammed his fist on the table and yelled, "Dammit! That's enough."

One of them said, "You swore!"

"You're damn right I did."

The anger in his voice made me admire his honesty. I reached over and touched his arm. "Thanks for being real!"

No one said anything for a minute or two, and finally I added, "I don't know what you're going through. I'm willing to listen. I'll pray for you. I'll try to be available whenever you want to talk, or you think I can help."

Jeff choked up with tears, but he didn't say anything.

The other three men tried to console Jeff. One of them started a new sermon, but I held up my hand. "He's heard enough. He doesn't want your answers; he wants your compassion."

I don't remember much about the next ten minutes before we dispersed. To his credit, the man with the iPad grabbed Jeff's lunch check.

Since then Jeff has jumped from one job to another. His present position earns him about 60 percent of what he earned before. Jeff is now living "after this." Is he now healthier, stronger, more mature?

Maybe, although I haven't seen much evidence of a positive life change.

So why do I relate these two stories? Because often when we want to help others, we speak out of *our* discomfort and perhaps *our* fear. We can't focus on the Jeffs around us because we're really thinking of ourselves.

My hurting friends don't need my advice;
they need my compassion.

23

Living in Empty Spaces

NOW, YEARS LATER, I still look back and consider the time after the white flight when I was forty-one and jobless as the most painful time in my work life. I had what we'd call today "a severance package" that paid my salary for up to one year. The problem wasn't the money; the problem was that I had no job.

During that time, I lived in a kind of vacuum. I was no longer who I had been and didn't know who I was going to become. In the American dream, productivity not only counted but also defined me. So for nine months I didn't know who I was.

That was the empty space—the place where I couldn't go back to what I had done and the doors hadn't opened to where I could start fresh. So I talked to friends and contacts and did all the good things that jobless people do.

The fourth month of emptiness was so difficult that I ended up in the hospital with an ulcer. I was back home in two days without surgery, but it was an insightful time for me.

I had to ask myself serious questions, such as:

- *If I don't function the way I used to, am I still of value?*
- *What will I do if no one ever hires me?*
- *Will I end up taking a menial, low-paying job just to survive?*
  (I had two master's degrees and had done a year's study
  in a PhD program.)

That painful experience and the tough questions forced me to accept the emptiness of my life. I was a normal American male, a husband with three children, and well educated.

But I had failed. Or at least not having a job implied failure.

People would have understood had I gone to another pastorate while our church prepared to die, but I couldn't do that. I felt I had to stay for the funeral and the grieving afterward. In the midst of others' pain and sadness, I had to figure out who I was and what I wanted to do with my life.

I was a normal American male, a husband with three children, and well educated. *But I had failed.* Or at least not having a job implied failure.

I struggled through those months, trying to make sense of my life when it seemed to make no sense. I prayed, and I agonized. I searched my heart to ask if I had done something wrong to bring about the awful situation. Nothing changed.

Eventually I came to a conclusion. It wasn't what I had done for a living that defined me. I liked what I did, but it wasn't my entire life.

About the eighth month, I was no closer to a job. Although months earlier I had been interviewed by one search committee and felt it would have been an excellent fit, I didn't hear from them again. I also had three interviews where churches wanted me to become their pastor, but none of them seemed to fit me, so I turned them down.

I finally figured out that I had to use the time to make sense out of my emptiness and to focus on who I was and not concentrate strictly on my vocation.

Who was I?

What did I want?

Those were such difficult questions to face, but staring right at them became the changing point. I used the vacuum as a time for self-exploration. I pondered the question, *What do I want to do with the rest of my life?* I had to decide what was important to me, regardless of job opportunities (or lack of them). I finally worked through the questions. Slowly, peace came over me.

At the beginning of my ninth month, representatives from the church I had liked contacted me again. They explained they had internal issues to take care of before they were ready to talk seriously to me.

They came on a Sunday morning to hear me when I was the guest speaker at a different church. From there, the process we refer to as the "calling of a minister" usually takes weeks. It took six hours. That same Sunday afternoon an elder phoned to ask if I would meet with them that evening.

Who was I?
What did I want?

They asked questions, I answered, and in slightly less than one hour, the leading elder asked, "Will you accept a call to become our pastor?"

I accepted and stayed ten years. And they were the best years of my work as a pastor.

The reason they were the best years was because I had learned invaluable lessons about living in the emptiness. I was able to function as a pastor, but that role didn't fully define me. It declared what I did, but I was more than my role.

I had started to publish three years earlier. Those ten years at that church became my most productive as a writer. Even though I wrote only one hour (sometimes two) before my secretary arrived each morning, my writing was freer and, I think, better. I wrote from who I was and was able to share as much of myself as I knew of myself.

I need the empty spaces in life
to learn to accept fullness in life.

24

Marked Faces

I STARED AT THE WRINKLES in the old man's face. He seemed to have more wrinkles than anyone I—as a ten-year-old—had ever seen before. I reached up and touched him. "Feels funny," I said.

He smiled before he said, "Those are my marks." Aware that I didn't understand, he added, "Each of these lines tells you about me. It's the way my face has kept score." He took my hand and we traced another wrinkle. He explained what it was from, then we moved on to another.

I realize now that he was teasing me, yet there was a great deal of truth in what he said. He was a marked man.

All of us are marked by our experiences. The lines or gray hair express the aging process, but our markings are also on the inside. We know the effects of pain, rejection, humiliation, and failure. For example, sometimes I'll see a movie with someone whose age is late fifties but the person looks at least twenty years older. Someone will usually say something like "She's done a lot of hard living" or "His lifestyle tells on him."

But we also know the marks of success. When fitness expert Jack Lalanne died at age ninety-six, my fifty-seven-year-old friend said, "I wish I looked that good right now."

The point I want to make is that life marks us. We're marked by our inner scars and empowered by our experiences and the things we've learned. Once we've gone through chaos, confusion, or a time when life doesn't make sense, we will be changed in some way.

As we get older, of course, we define those interior marks as *wisdom* or *insight*—and they are. But they also reflect the wounds of being human and living on this planet. The more intense the trauma and the more certain we were that we wouldn't survive, the greater the scars on our psyche. Some people never get beyond those scars.

For example, my parents were caught in the Great Depression in the 1930s. They were farmers during the Dust Bowl years as well, and they never forgot those days. Although they both lived more than fifty years after those experiences, they were marked. No matter how much money Dad had or how debt free they had become, they constantly acted as they had in 1935.

We're marked by our inner scars and empowered by our experiences and the things we've learned.

Almost every time I ate at home, my mother announced it was time to eat with these words, "Eat up, because you don't know when you'll have another meal." My parents were long past that kind of poverty, but they couldn't forget.

One time I said to Mom, "You always say that."

She told me that if I had gone through what she had, I'd say it too. She told me it was her way of being thankful for what she had now. She said there were days when she had no food, and many times she worked all day for a potato or a bowl of soup. She was afraid then, and she would never forget that feeling.

But not all marks disfigure our psyches or minds. They can also enhance our lives and change us for the better. We're all marked in some way. We can focus on the hardness of life or that the nation has gone downhill and morals have degenerated. Or we can focus on the goodness of life, the kindness of others.

As I thought of the old man with wrinkles (and I now have them myself), I remember that Shirley used to point to people who had, in her words, "laugh wrinkles."

Their faces reflected a happy, positive view of life.

Lord, give me a lot of laugh wrinkles.

I'm being marked.
My markings reflect who I am becoming.

25

Ends and Beginnings

"YOU TOOK THE END of that job too seriously," my neighbor said to my friend Gene. "You acted as if it was final—"

"It was," Gene protested.

"No, it was the end of *that* episode, but your life will be filled with many endings. Get used to it!"

The conversation didn't involve me, so I said nothing; however, despite the abruptness of my neighbor's words, he was right. Gene was twenty-two years old and had been on his first full-time job a year when his boss fired him. I felt the boss was unreasonable, and he yelled so loud that Gene never had an opportunity to speak a word in his own defense.

"You're fired. Get out!"

"It's over," Gene said to me, "but..."

The *but* was the warning sign that it wasn't over. As long as Gene replayed the "conversation" in his head and figured out ways to explain or to yell louder than his former employer, it wasn't over.

When we go through unpleasant experiences, especially when we feel we've been wronged, it's difficult to dismiss the situation. We tell ourselves it's the end, but it doesn't feel the way an ending should.

Because we haven't resolved the issues, we hang on—we cling to the end and refuse to let the experience die.

I had a similar response when I was the ghostwriter for a celebrity and we had nearly finished the book. On what turned out to be my final visit to see him, he acted odd, as if he had pulled back from me. Until then he had been remarkably open.

He isn't the kind of person I could ask, "Is something wrong?" and get an answer. He couldn't confront anyone and always had his secretary do the unpleasant tasks.

A week after my visit, I called his office, couldn't get him (which wasn't unusual), and left a message. He didn't return the call; his secretary didn't return the call. I called once more with the same results. I never did learn what was wrong or what I had or hadn't done to offend him.

I received all the money to which I was entitled, but the ending was abrupt and rude. In my mind, I struggled with the situation, even though I knew it was over. The editor didn't know the reason either, or at least said he didn't, but I couldn't let go of the pain for a long time.

Even if it's over—whether a job loss, a love affair, a marriage, or anything else—as long as we continue to focus on what was, what might have been, or what we could have done to prevent the end, it's not over.

In my case, for several months whenever that celebrity's name came up, I had to fight not to spew out my anger. I kept holding on, wanting to justify my behavior or at least have an explanation so I could defend myself. I didn't like being angry, but I was. And one day I admitted that I hadn't been ready to say it was done. Finished.

For a long time I carried the "end" of that around inside me. I had never been fired from a book project like that. Finally I was able to admit it was over and put it behind me.

By contrast, years ago, I had a strong argument with a man named

Bud. It was probably the angriest I've ever been. For a long time I nursed the painful words he spoke and thought of dozens of ways I might have bested him with my response.

One day I wrote him and asked him to forgive me for anything I'd done to offend him. He wrote back and asked me to forgive him as well. That letter ushered in a peaceful ending.

> As long as we continue to focus on what was, what might have been, or what we could have done to prevent the end, it's not over.

As I wrote this chapter, I tried to recall exactly what we had said to each other. His accusations hurt so deeply I was positive I'd never forget them. But I have. Honestly.

I know we argued. I know also that a woman carried gossip from him to me and from me to him, which caused the conflict. Even so, truthfully, I can't remember what we fought about.

And that has enabled me to know when something is finished and gone: *I forget.* As long as I can vividly describe the pain and give anyone a fairly close approximation of our conversation, I'm still imprisoned by the past. The ending hasn't come.

This principle works, regardless of the messy circumstances. As long as we can recall specifically what the boss did, how the corporation treated us, how the church leader failed us, or how one of our children turned from us—we're still living with unfinished business. Until we let go, we're hanging on to our pain, our hurt, our betrayal, and our anger.

Sometimes the present is really the past that I won't release. As long as I relive the pain, it's not over.

26

"If Only I Had..."

I MADE A FEW SMART DECISIONS by the time I was twenty. One of the wisest was I promised myself that I wouldn't come to the end of life, look backward, and say, "If only I had..."

That resolution came to me when I was in the military on shore patrol duty—which happened about once every six weeks—and the officer in charge assigned me to the enlisted men's club that night.

My tasks were to make sure no one got into trouble and to stop anyone who showed signs of intoxication. In the eight times I did that duty, I was bored and never had problems with anyone. Occasionally, however, I had a conversation with one of the sailors.

One night a man sat drinking beer and talking to no one. After his fifth beer, I walked over and said hello. My armband made it obvious I was on duty, and I wanted to be sure he was still sober.

When he started talking about himself, I realized he was lonely.

"Ten months and eight days to go," he told me as he hoisted the bottle to his lips.

"Before you ship out?" I asked.

He shook his head and showed me the three red hash marks

on his uniform—each representing four years. "Instead of getting a fourth one, I'm cashing out."

We talked for a few minutes—mostly he talked. I don't know if he was almost drunk or was just sentimental. I finally asked, "What do you plan to do once you're out?"

"I don't know," he said. "I don't know." He told me he had always wanted to be a gym teacher, but he never went to college.

When I suggested he go to college with his G.I. educational benefits, he shook his head. "Too old."

For the next ten or fifteen minutes he talked to me about the bad decisions he had made. He had a life of terrible regrets. He had stayed in the navy because it was easy and all he had to do "was keep my head down, salute officers, and not get caught." He had loved a girl in his hometown, but months after he enlisted, she married someone else. "I've been married twice, but she's the only one I really loved."

As I listened to him going back to what he wished he had done with his life, that's when I resolved I would never reach the place in my life where I said, "If only I had..."

Nearly thirty years later, my son, John Mark, joined a country band and played guitar. He had taken lessons for a couple of years and, to my untrained ear, his playing seemed good. The group called themselves Harvest South, and they got bookings most weekends.

John Mark seemed a little unsure about doing it, but I encouraged him to try. I reminded him that if he didn't make it big, he could always say, "I tried." Specifically, I said, "Don't ever come to the end of your life and wish you had gone for it."

He did stay with the band and even sang a few solos. For a couple of years the band did well. Then John Mark quit. By then he had married, and they had a daughter. He told me he left the band because he wanted to spend more time with his wife and daughter. What he said was true—at least part of the truth. Two decades later he told me, "I was good on the guitar; but I wasn't great. That's the other reason I stopped."

I applauded him. He'll never have to regret what he didn't try.

If it's something you truly want to do—even if you try and fail—do it anyway. Don't come to the end of your life and say, "If only I had…"

We all have regrets about the things we've done. But the biggest regrets are about the things we didn't do.

27

Starting Over

HERE ARE TWO FACTS: First, anyone can start over. Second, everyone has trouble with starting over.

We may eagerly look forward to starting over, yet something in us resists doing it, as if we are taking the first step toward disaster. We all have different anxieties and uncertainties, but they arise from the fear that starting over destroys the old ways.

We are afraid that change will destroy the idea of who we are and what we need. To start again means we have to leave some or all of that behind.

- "I used to be a housewife, but now I'm a receptionist."
- "I defined myself as a motivational speaker, and now I'm trying to define myself as a teacher in the public schools."
- "I used to be a husband, but now I'm single."

We're not always aware of those feelings. But something— some hidden anxiety—wants to hold us back.

After I had been a pastor for fourteen years, I decided to take the risk of writing full-time in spite of the statistics that only about

2 percent of writers make a living just at writing. I knew I'd never be content unless I took the step.

Did those uncertainties and anxieties pull at me? Of course.

I had discovered what I truly wanted to do. Even though I was aware of how deeply I wanted to move into my new career, it took me eight or nine months to make that decision.

I wrestled with feelings of self-doubt, such as whether I was good enough to make a successful transition. Did I have enough book ideas to get started? Would I still have ideas in ten years?

I had to figure out what undermined my resolve to start over in a new career. The more I researched, the more discouraging the information seemed, but I couldn't give it up. The congregation continued to grow and I wasn't forced to leave the pastorate.

Yet I couldn't escape the desire to write. I also began to tire of what I had once loved doing—visiting homes, teaching, preaching, and interacting with a variety of people throughout the day.

One day I asked myself, *If I remain a pastor, is it something that will satisfy me for the rest of my professional life?*

> I had to figure out what undermined my resolve to start over in a new career.

I knew it wouldn't. From that moment on, I started to move forward. Each step seemed extremely difficult. I thought of the people I wouldn't see again after I left; I felt anxious about shut-ins and didn't know if the interim pastor would visit them. I had started a study group for men, and I knew it wouldn't continue if I left. I was the one who pushed for more community involvement through helping people with rent or food.

To my surprise, when I looked back, money wasn't an issue. I sensed I could do it. My wife worked, and we could pay our essential bills with her check even if I sold nothing.

Most of all, however, I realized that my old way of life (being a pastor) no longer satisfied my creative urges. I loved writing sermons, even though I didn't preach them as written. I wrote a column for a weekly newspaper and enjoyed that.

The most significant question over which I wrestled was simple: *Do I like myself well enough to be alone all day?* That question may seem trivial and silly to some, but it wasn't to me. As I surveyed my working life, I had always been in jobs that involved people and interworking with them. I was moving into a solitary profession.

More than once I took the Myers Briggs Type Indicator, a personality test. Each time I came out high on the extroverted side. That wasn't a good indicator for someone who would move into a solitary occupation.

I struggled, I questioned, and I did it. I resigned.

Did I like myself well enough to be alone? Probably not at first, but I grew comfortable with who I was.

I started over.

A few months later, I looked back and asked myself, *What took you so long?*

Because it's difficult to start over doesn't make it impossible or mean I've made a mistake. It means I've taken a risk, and I'm willing to try something new.

28

The Same Mistakes

MY BROTHER MEL WAS MARRIED five times. I served as best man the first time, and I met the next two women before he married them. Mel didn't talk a lot about personal things, especially his feelings, but he did say the first time, "I love her. I plan to stay married to her forever."

He said that at his second marriage and his third. I wasn't around for wives four and five. My brother had problems—many problems—and he kept repeating the same patterns, wondering later what had gone wrong.

Mel became a drunk. But once when he was sober and had just married for the fifth time, I asked him, "Don't you feel guilty over all those divorces?"

He shook his head. "I just block them out of my mind and they're gone. I move on."

He may have done exactly that. Perhaps that's why he failed so often at marriage. But instead of blocking out mistakes or unwise decisions, we can use them as an excellent opportunity to pause, to reflect, and to make sense out of life.

In one of Mel's maudlin, half-stupor moments, he once asked me (it was probably rhetorical), "Why does all this bad stuff happen to me?"

I don't recall what I answered, but I do remember that he took another swig of his beer and talked next about needing new tires on his car.

I wish he could have said, "This has happened before. What makes me continue to repeat the same patterns?"

And it's not just my brother. I've seen this with many people—even talented people who "ought" to have been successful.

More than twenty years ago I worked for a short time with Cynthia, a high-powered, talented publicist. Sometimes she'd call and tell me about a really big deal (*big* was her word for megabucks), but something always went wrong before signing the contract.

> Instead of blocking out mistakes or unwise decisions, we can use them as an excellent opportunity to pause, to reflect, and to make sense out of life.

I have a friend named Sam who seems always to self-sabotage his opportunities. Twice he's tried to talk me into investing with him, and both times I refused. He made great promises, and none of them were ever as fruitful as he said they would be. Many of them failed.

Sam kept making the same mistakes—and, even from far away, to me they were obvious. He didn't keep clients informed; he ignored them until he was ready to talk. Once I said, "When people invest money, they have a right to know what you're doing."

"I'll tell them when I'm ready," he said.

I couldn't understand that. He couldn't seem to grasp that by putting a little effort into communication, he could save his business ventures. The last time I saw him, which was about two years ago, he was working on a project that he was certain would make him enough money to retire.

Our mistakes don't have to be that big. They can be small ones that hold us back from more intimacy or from high productivity levels.

But large or small, we tend to have the same pattern: we keep repeating, hoping we'll get it right the next time. We rarely do.

We can change the pattern. It won't take much for us to figure out the reason we make the mistakes. And we'll do it if we want to succeed.

If it happened once,
I can change so that it doesn't happen again.

29

What We Didn't Get...

I RECENTLY WROTE AN E-MAIL to a hurting friend who suffers from the effects of terrible things he's done to others. I'm sorry for his pain, but I'm delighted he's facing himself. It takes courage to look at ourselves and admit that we committed acts we condemn in others. (In fact, condemning others for those very acts is often the way many try to cope with their own issues.)

I was the victim of childhood physical and sexual abuse. When I faced that, I learned an invaluable lesson. I don't know if I read it, someone told me, or if God whispered it to me, but here's the lesson: *What we don't receive in childhood, we spend our lives seeking—usually on an unconscious level.* Like most people, I focused on the symptoms and tried not to do things I knew were wrong. Years ago, while visiting an AA meeting, I heard the term *dry alcoholic,* and that sums it up for me. Dry alcoholics no longer drink, but they haven't altered their attitudes. They don't change because they still haven't resolved their issues.

I figured out that *unacceptable behavior* (a nice term to cover compulsive problems) is a painkiller. My dad and brothers killed their pain with beer. I remember a woman who was the most notorious gossip I've ever known; many times I've thought that carrying the latest news (true or not) gave her a sense of feeling significant, perhaps even important. The "medicine" each of them took for temporary relief probably worked—temporarily.

Most of us didn't have a fully happy childhood, and that's where the problems began. We didn't get everything we wanted or needed. Some of those things weren't significant, but if we didn't feel wanted or cared about back then, we will spend much (or perhaps all) of our life trying to find love or to feel wanted by someone.

The worst part of my childhood was that I never felt loved. Because of that, I tried all kinds of ways to be cared for and accepted by others. I befriended a lot of kids when I was in school. It was my unconscious attempt to get from them what I hadn't gotten at home.

The worst part of my childhood was that I never felt loved.

As I write this chapter, the name *Laura Bish* jumps into my mind. She was the poorest student in our class and seemed to have only two dresses to wear to school.

Sometimes I walked home from school with her (it was on my way). After my friend Ronnie Larson teased me about it, I tried to get her to walk fast so the other kids wouldn't see us.

One time I tried to help Laura with her spelling, but she couldn't seem to remember how to spell even simple words.

But most of all, I remember Valentine's Day. I was the only person in our classroom who gave her a valentine. When I realized she wasn't going to get others, I had extras with me so I scribbled her name and tried to disguise my handwriting. Then I passed them to kids around me. Because they had Laura's name on the envelope, they passed them to her. She received five cards...all from me.

Why did I do that? If you had asked me then, I wouldn't have known. As I look back, I think the reason I reached out to her in friendship and kindness was because that was what I wanted to receive.

So as strange as it may seem, I had a number of odd friends—often the class outcasts or those who didn't seem to fit in. By giving to them, I was seeking to be loved and wanted.

I also remember what happened when I turned fifteen. I had never had a birthday party, although I had attended several. That year I asked a friend if we could use his house for a party. I didn't tell anyone the occasion, but I bought an inexpensive gift for each guest.

Strange behavior, yes. Doing for others what no one did for me was one way I tried—unknowingly—to reach out for love and acceptance. Later, with the help of God and my wife and my best friend, I was able to receive and to feel genuinely loved.

What I don't receive in childhood
I spend my life seeking.

30

Shaped by Waiting

WHEN WE HAD OUR FIRST CHILD, Wanda—even more than the two born later—everything in our lives seemed to revolve around her birth. Exercise and diet played a large part in the way Shirley took care of herself while pregnant.

I was careful that Shirley didn't get overly tired or try to do too much. Waiting for our daughter's birth shaped much of our lives during those months.

Recently I heard an interview with a man imprisoned for twenty-three years for a crime he didn't commit before DNA testing proved his innocence. In the interview, he said the worst part in his confinement was after he knew he was going to be released. "I still had to wait. Hours seemed to go by slowly." He didn't say how long, but the implication was that he had to remain incarcerated about a month for state officials to complete all the paperwork.

Imagine the inner turmoil as he hung around his cell. He was soon to be a free man, but in the meantime he waited. And waited.

It sounds strange to say it that way, but it's a fact of life: we are shaped by waiting around until something good or bad happens.

What if you've lost your job and have sent out résumés? Suppose you're going through a divorce. Your spouse doesn't want to be married to you yet seems to use every delay tactic to stop the filing of the papers. Perhaps you'll have your college degree in four weeks, and you already have five job interviews set up—but all of them will take place only after you hold your degree in hand. Remember when you were only nineteen days from being old enough to get a driver's license?

In each of these instances, you waited. And much of life revolves around doing nothing. Being unable to move forward.

Part of who we are now is a result of how we responded while we waited. The waiting shapes us so we either learn to relax or we grow impatient and perhaps even angry. We waste energy saying, "If only..." We blame others because we have to stand in line at the pharmacy or wait for the nurse to lead us to the doctor's office.

Sometimes I've heard people refer to "killing time." That strong image denotes an extremely negative sense of what we do as we wait for the anticipated event.

I'm sure there are many ways to stay in place with resentment or displeasure. Any of those work because they consume our thoughts and our energy. But they don't make us better, stronger, or happier.

Or we can learn to think, *This is life. Everything doesn't happen on my schedule.*

I'm not good at waiting, but I'm getting better at it. And, like everyone I know, I've certainly had enough practice. I try to anticipate waiting. I'm a reader and nearly always carry a book with me when I have an appointment, whether I'm going to the doctor, meeting a friend for lunch, getting a haircut, or attending a business meeting.

> Part of who we are now depends on how we responded while we waited.

But even more important than having something to occupy my mind, I'm aware of what waiting does to us. *Marking time* is another negative expression that implies nothing happens.

But something *does* happen. We either learn to accept that not getting immediate action is a significant part of life, or we resent anyone or anything that impedes us from direct action. If we pay attention, we gain a little insight into who we are.

I caught on to this last week as I waited in line to check out two books at the library. There were two checkout computers and two or three clerks behind the desk, but that Thursday afternoon the library was filled with patrons (as they call us).

As I waited my turn, I decided not to grumble about waiting—after all, the other patrons wanted to check out books to read and (I hoped) to improve their minds. They had as much right to be waited on as I did—and they got in line before me.

I also thought, *If I didn't have to wait, I would probably get out of this building about four minutes earlier. How much difference would that make in my life?*

I'm reminded of the words of Jesus, who said, "Can all your worries add a single moment to your life?"[3]

Rather than worrying, fretting, feeling anxious, I'm learning (still learning) to relax and simply be glad I'm still healthy, alive, and able to be there to wait.

I am shaped by waiting,
and I can shape the waiting into a positive experience.

31

Missing the Meaning

I HAVE A THEORY ABOUT our experiences, especially when the same results occur repeatedly. For instance, Evelyn has had two bad marriages, and she's getting ready to marry for the third time. I hardly know the man, but I expect this relationship to end up in divorce as well.

Jason has changed jobs repeatedly during the past five years. Here are some of his statements:

- "The boss wasn't fair. He let other people get away with things."
- "I worked as hard as anyone else, but I wasn't going to nice-up to my supervisor like the others did."
- "I do my job, and I don't think I ought to clean up the area for other people who are just too lazy to do it themselves."

Most of us have heard about the Evelyns and the Jasons from our neighbors or our friends. Sometimes we think, *Will she ever learn? Why doesn't he get it?* But we rarely say anything. On those few occasions when we have spoken up, we've been rebuffed, ignored, or belittled. Usually others are good at telling us why we're wrong or letting us know that we have no idea how difficult life is for them.

So here's my theory: We keep running into the same type of situations until we learn the lessons we need. Evelyn keeps marrying abusive men. All three are different in looks and jobs, but she has an uncanny ability to be attracted to men who batter her.

T. S. Eliot is credited with these words: "We had the experience but missed the meaning." We may go through dark places (or good ones), but if nothing changes in us, the experience was useless.

We can learn and grow from each experience. That is, if we're willing to learn. I'm reminded of an experience with my son, John Mark. When he was ten years old, he complained that his teacher had not done something right. After he explained, I assumed he was probably correct, but it wasn't worth a confrontation with his teacher.

"Life isn't always fair," I said, "and you can count this as a learning experience."

"I've already learned too many lessons," our son said.

It was a jovial retort and both of us laughed, but his immature response is what I hear at times from forty-year-old men and women. They don't see such events as life lessons but only as more struggles and greater problems.

We can learn and grow from each experience. That is, if we're willing to learn.

Years ago I stumbled on to the importance of this concept. In a two-year period, I had been hospitalized twice with an ulcer. The second time I asked myself, *What is going on that makes me need to be sick?* (I had learned not to ask why. That question seeks analytical answers but doesn't change anything even if we know the answer.)

I also asked it this way: *What makes me want to be sick?* Since then I've expanded that question. Now when I face difficulties or opposition, I ask myself, *What do I need to learn from this?*

My theory is that if I don't get the life lesson from this experience, that's all right. A similar situation will come up again.

And again.

And again.

Until I catch the meaning, I'll continue to have such experiences.

Here's a good question to ask myself:
What is going on inside me
that makes me need this mess?

32

Remembering Correctly?

WE DON'T REMEMBER EVENTS ACCURATELY. Or maybe we unconsciously reinterpret what we remember. I don't think it's dishonesty; I do think it's a natural phenomenon.

I became aware of this many years ago when I heard people talk about their conversion experience. Usually it was their awareness of moving from unbelief to faith. Sometimes it involved a moment of enlightenment when they realized they needed to start a fitness program, leave a marriage, or quit smoking.

Although this is true with everyday experiences, I'd like to explore this from the big moments—the kind of thing where we say, "I'll never forget this," or, "It is so imprinted on my memory it's as if it happened only hours ago."

Sounds good, but that's not true, at least from my experience and observation.

Relating a conversion experience, the way they told it was greatly influenced *by the closeness of the time to the experience.*

For example, when people speak of meeting God for the first time and it happened recently, their theology may be off, or they might be unclear on how to relate their experience. The language is usually raw. That is, they know something powerful happened, but they have difficulty articulating it; however, their passion usually makes up for their inadequacy of being able to explain it.

But if we meet those same people a year later, or ten years later, they don't tell the same story. The core is probably the same: they went from ignorance to enlightenment, from doubt to faith, from feeling lost to feeling found. But if we listen carefully, we realize that they've added to the original message.

They now speak in retrospect—naturally—but there is a significant difference. They've learned lessons since then. They've realized the experience was even more powerful than they first thought. Or perhaps it has become less significant.

The way we remember the past says a great deal about who we are now. How do I see myself in the events now, compared to the way I saw myself at an earlier time?

This is significant to me as a ghostwriter or collaborator. When I do autobiographies, I believe the subjects of the books are being as truthful as they can be. After the publication of any autobiography, family members often quietly dispute the facts. "That's not the way I remember it," one woman said about her sister's book.

So which sister was correct? My answer: probably neither, if we look at something we might call *literal fact.*

Yet both are accurate. They interpreted the experience or event according to their own understanding of themselves or of the world. And that interpretation reflects their current life more than it does when it actually happened.

I'll illustrate this by writing about how I got involved in a regular

fitness program. After I had been hospitalized with ulcers twice, the doctor told
me I had become a chronic ulcer patient
so he would need to see me regularly. I
left his office determined that I would
never have to return. (I haven't.) That
led me into an ongoing fitness program.

> The way we remember the past says a great deal about who we are now.

Those are the bare facts. At the time I kept a journal and recorded part of what the doctor told me. Nine years later I read the account and realized that, although I kept the essence of the story, the details varied. As I remembered it, I began an exercise program the next day—I was sure of it. My journal said it was several weeks later.

About four months after that I drastically changed my eating habits, yet I was sure I did it within three or four days. There are a few other discrepancies too, but I hope I've made my point.

One final thing is that *how* or *what* we "remember" may be as important as the event itself. Because I place a high value on physical fitness and healthy eating, I "remember" moving into a healthy lifestyle almost immediately. The end effect was the same, but the experience wasn't quite as immediate.

Someone recently sent me a quotation by Alan Wright that goes along with this: "The way you remember yesterday determines how you will live tomorrow."

He said it better than I could.

When I speak of the past, I say, "This is how I remember it," even though I've unconsciously added my current perception to an old memory.

33

"I Just Want to Be Happy"

RAYMOND CAME INTO MY OFFICE and, within seconds of sitting down, he dropped his head into his hands and started to cry.

He had phoned that morning and asked if I would stay at my office until five thirty so he could talk to me. I had agreed to wait.

He wasn't a man I knew well. I was his pastor, and he attended regularly, although he rarely participated in any congregational activities. I'd seen men cry before, so that didn't disturb me. I came from behind my desk and sat in a chair facing him, our knees about six inches apart. I stared at him and waited.

"I just want to be happy," he said. "Is that too much to ask in life?" He continued to cry.

Finally he told me of problems in his marriage. "We yell at each other almost every day, and I'm tired of it."

His job also wasn't going well because the company was expanding, and the executives were pressuring him to put in more time.

As he talked about the messes in his life, he jumped from one topic to another and kept coming back to being happy. "I just want to enjoy life. I don't ask too much. I don't need a million dollars—" And he went into a litany of what he didn't need.

I don't like giving advice to people, even though it sometimes seems obvious what they need. But after Raymond spent at least half an hour talking and kept coming back to his single theme, I decided it was time to speak.

I leaned over and laid both my hands on his. For the first time he looked directly at me. "Stop looking for happiness," I said.

That statement shocked him. "So I should live in misery—"

I pulled back and raised my hand. "No, you've made happiness your focus, and I think you're wrong. You simply want to feel good."

"What's wrong with feeling good?"

I shook my head. "Happiness doesn't work that way. If you seek it, you'll never find it."

He swore at me, asking if I was trying to play a head game with him.

I thought for a minute and said I honestly didn't think I was. "Happiness is a result of choices—the right choices—" and I stopped him before he could interrupt me. "What makes you feel fulfilled? What gives you pleasure?"

He thought for a few minutes and didn't seem to know. "I enjoy some things, but I'm not happy."

> "Stop looking for happiness," I said. That statement shocked him.

He stayed perhaps about twenty minutes longer and said he felt better before he left. I'm not certain he did. If we constantly ask ourselves, *Am I happy?* we'll find reasons we're not.

But if we can say, "I want to live life. I want to enjoy it," it may surprise us one day to realize we actually are happy.

If I look for happiness, it eludes me;
if I accept and enjoy what I have, happiness finds me.

34

What Makes Us Happy?

DAVID MORGAN CALLED ME AFTER he had watched the trailer for a documentary. A person with a handheld camera interviewed people on the street. He asked each of them one simple question with exactly these words: "What would make you happy?"

As expected, the answers were typical:

- "Pay off my debts."
- "Get a better job."
- "Own a mortgage-free house with a pool."

After each person answered, the man with the camera turned the question around and asked, "What makes you happy?"

Those same people responded with

- "Enjoying the beautiful weather."
- "Listening to soft music."
- "Spending time with my loved ones."

Replacing the verb *would make* with *makes* altered the question and brought out different answers because the responses came from a different part of the individuals.

To the first question, "What would make you happy?" their replies were external—changing the situation or receiving a large sum of money...always something outside of their being and beyond their immediate grasp.

Many people look "out there" and fantasize about things they'll probably never have. It's the same kind of talk when people tell me what they'll do if they win the lottery. When I was a boy, people would say, "When my ship comes in, I'll..." The language has changed but not the thinking. As the man with the camera suggested in his documentary, people say having those "things" will make them happy.

They don't have "it," so they don't know how they'll react. Although some individuals probably think that way, my assumption is that many of them mean, "I'd enjoy my life a lot more if..." But they're still talking about something they don't have or haven't experienced.

By contrast, when I ponder the many good things in my life, I realize that many influences impinge on us to make us want more and more. Each time, the implied message is, "If you have this one item, you'll be happy."

The rephrased question turns us inward. Instead of looking at what might be, we reflect seriously on our lives as they are right now. The question becomes one of these:

- "What do you most enjoy?"
- "What makes you content?"
- "What makes life worth living?"

The rephrasing forces us to look internally: What makes me happy *now*? The question implies that there is something already active in us and, with a little reflection, we can value life and appreciate being alive. The answer is already inside us. Our happiness doesn't come about because of our surroundings or circumstances.

Many influences impinge on us to make us want more and more. Each time, the implied message is, "If you have this one item, you'll be happy."

Years ago I used to hear missionaries speak disparagingly about people in the unindustrialized nations. "They are so content with the simple lives they have." The Westerners implied that if the nationals became more aware of the world beyond them, they would realize that their uncomplicated lifestyle was inferior.

I never agreed with that. I admire the people who seem to have few possessions, yet enjoy themselves. I like what St. Paul wrote to his protégé Timothy:

Yet true godliness with contentment is itself great wealth. After all, we brought nothing with us when we came into the world, and we can't take anything with us when we leave it. So if we have enough food and clothing, let us be content.[4]

Paul also wrote a letter to a European church at a place called Philippi. At the time he wrote, he was in prison, wrongly accused by his enemies, but he bore no bitterness. While he was imprisoned, members of that congregation sent him a gift, which he doesn't identify. He thanks them profusely and adds,

> Not that I was ever in need, for I have learned how to be content with whatever I have. I know how to live on almost nothing or with everything. I have learned the secret of living in every situation, whether it is with a full stomach or empty, with plenty or with little.[5]

Part of our growth is to find pleasure and experience deep peace in appreciating what we already have.

I don't need more things to be happy;
I need to value what I already have.

35

Glass Jaws

THE MANAGER WATCHED THE NEWSREEL and had one segment replayed several times. "There! Stop the film!" He pointed to the screen and said to his fighter, the film's hero, "See for yourself! He's got a glass jaw!"

As a boy watching the movie, I didn't get the meaning of *glass jaw*— at least not at first. He pointed out that the other fighter wouldn't let anyone hit his face. He seemed able to handle any kind of body blow, but he protected his jaw and nose.

The manager had picked out the weak place—the soft spot— of the opponent and gloated. When the big fight came on screen, the hero went for the man's face and battered it relentlessly. When his opponent put his hands up to protect his face, the hero threw heavy blows to the stomach. As soon as the glass-jawed fighter's hands came down, the hero went for the face again.

When the fight ended, the glass-jawed fighter lay unconscious on the canvas while the crowd cheered.

In the film they kept calling it "the glass jaw," and I've sometimes heard it referred to as "the soft spot." It's the place where we're sensitive, where we're easily hurt or deflated.

It's also the place where we usually become defensive. That is, we'll do whatever we can to protect the place where we're vulnerable and others are able to hurt us.

We all have the soft spots, and as long as they remain, we'll automatically switch into a defensive mode to protect ourselves. Someone challenges a statement we've made or laughs at the way we speak. We work on a presentation, and our manager scoffs at our work and calls it simplistic.

We don't outgrow the glass jaw, but we can learn to overcome it. For instance, I love to sing and often go around the house doing just that. Yet I honestly can't sing well. It took me a long time to realize that because my voice sounded all right to me.

> We all have the soft spots, and as long as they remain, we'll automatically switch into a defensive mode to protect ourselves.

It wasn't that I defended myself, but sometimes I sulked or felt wounded when someone commented on my voice. But after I finally admitted that I can't stay on pitch, the victory was in sight. The problem isn't having the soft spot; it's the need to protect that weak place.

Nowadays when people occasionally make fun of my singing, my answer is simple. "It's the best I can do."

I am learning to accept my weak spots.
The more readily I accept them,
the less energy I exert to protect them.

36

Struggling with Jealousy

NO MATTER WHO WE ARE, jealousy creeps into our lives. It's a natural response.

Someone gets a promotion that either we would like or don't feel the person deserves. Someone is honored for his work and we know we've worked as hard or perhaps harder. We feel like the girl who knew in third grade that she was the best speller and reader in the class, but the teacher awarded Sarah the gold star for being number one. Or the high schooler who worked harder than any teammate at learning to pitch, but the coach picked lazy Tom for captain—a guy who didn't care that much about the game.

The list goes on because we've all had our share of being ignored, rejected, or overlooked. We *know* we're more qualified, brighter, more experienced, more committed to the company...but someone else wins.

As a writer, I became aware of certain writers who had phenomenal success. I didn't think they were very good, and I was willing to show them or tell anyone who would listen why I was better. But their sales were larger and, in our culture, achievement is more important than quality or ability.

When I became aware of my jealousy—although it took me time to admit that's what it was—I had to do something to change my attitude.

I could resent them, store up negative thoughts about being discriminated against, rejoice when they had a failure, or even tell everyone how undeserving they were. I could do that—and yes, in shameful confession, I admit I did that a few times.

One day I realized I had a bad attitude, and my opinions didn't have any effect on the people of whom I was jealous. Their success had nothing to do with mine (or my lack of success).

About that time, several writers I had mentored moved into their first taste of success. I was genuinely happy for them. "You've worked for this," I said. "I'm delighted you've done it."

It seemed so inconsistent to me that I could be jealous of some and yet clap for others. I began to reason out the situation:

> One day I realized I had a bad attitude, and my opinions didn't have any effect on the people of whom I was jealous.

1. I wanted to be happy for everyone who succeeded.
2. I believed that some of them deserved rewards for their work.
3. I didn't know what went on inside the others whom I thought were less worthy.
4. Who was I to decide who was worthy and who wasn't?
5. If it pleased God to bless their efforts, who was I to tell God that it was wrong?
6. Jealousy was my way of stating my prejudice, but my feelings changed nothing.

With such thoughts in mind, I decided on the program that's often referred to as *fake-it-until-you-make-it*. I began to congratulate my friends (and even those I barely knew) on their accomplishments.

I can't point to a magic moment when the faking became the reality, but it happened. Perhaps one reason is because of how those so-called undeserving people responded. I didn't detect smugness or an attitude of "I worked for this, so I deserve it."

Their surprise at my words made me realize they were probably as insecure as I was. That helped me to joyfully respond to their achievements. I was able to say, "I'm happy for you."

Here's the strangest thing: the more I reached out to them and congratulated them, the more rapidly my jealousy departed. Not only did I learn to appreciate them, in some kind of unexplainable way, God decided to bless me even more. I'm not sure that it was a direct cause-and-effect situation, but I know I became different. My sales picked up and I sold more books, even though that wasn't the purpose for my change.

Today I can say with all candor that I'm genuinely happy for others in my profession. I want them to succeed. I struggled with jealousy (and once in a while twinges of it sneak into my mind before I banish it), but I've learned to enjoy others' successes.

To appreciate others' accomplishments
enables me to enjoy my own success.

37

The Messiness
of Anger

DAVID MORGAN IS THE BEST FRIEND I've ever known, and because of our friendship, I wanted to give him something special for Christmas. Although we've been close friends for a long time, gift exchange hasn't been part of our ritual. But one year I wanted to show an appreciation of him and our relationship.

Because I knew he liked chocolate ice cream, I assumed he'd enjoy chocolate candy. So I bought an expensive box of chocolates and took them to him.

"I don't eat chocolate candy," Dave said. He handed the box back to me unopened.

I stared at the wrapped package. I was hurt by his refusal. I felt angry and inside my head I called him ungrateful and thoughtless. I didn't say the words, but we did talk about it later. I also realized how angry I was.

It took me a few minutes to figure out why I was so upset. It came down to one word: *expectations*. While I thought about giving him the gift and wrapping it, my heart filled with mental images of his delight over receiving the unexpected present.

I anticipated something from Dave that he wasn't able to give me. He didn't live up to my expectations. Afterward I realized that was the reason for my anger. I had looked forward to his surprise and utter joy.

That's only one time when I struggled with the messiness of anger. But it was the beginning of understanding a powerful lesson. When I expect a particular response and don't receive it, I typically respond with heated words.

It seems so obvious to me now, but here are a few examples.

- I drove along a main highway, and a man pulled off a side street in front of me. I had to hit my brakes not to slam into him and yelled at him through my closed window. I had expected him to wait.

- A friend of mine had worked for a large corporation for almost a decade. His father was dying of inoperable prostate cancer. He visited the hospital on his way to work every morning. Because of traffic congestion, he was late for work two mornings in a row.

   His supervisor chewed him out for being late. (Think: supervisor's expectations.) Everyone in the office knew about my friend's dying father, so he yelled back at his supervisor for being such a jerk (except he used stronger words). (Think: he had expected understanding and sympathy, which he didn't get.)

- I followed a late-model Lexus that pulled in front of the kiosk at a parking lot. It was clearly marked for people to push a green button, receive a parking ticket, and then the gate would lift.

  The woman in front of me sat there, waiting. I beeped my horn lightly and received no response. A car pulled up behind me, and he also beeped. The attendant from the exit lane hurried over, pushed the button, and handed her a ticket. We waited again. I couldn't see, but I assume she was putting the ticket in her purse or something. Three horns blared behind me.

  All of us drivers behind the Lexus expected one form of behavior, and the woman didn't respond as we had anticipated.

Perhaps that's obvious, but I think it also gets even more complicated. We assume there is an obvious and particular standard of behavior. We believe in that rule and generally follow it. When we violate it, we feel we have valid reasons for doing so and forgive ourselves.

But we're not quite so willing to give another offending person the opportunity to live below our expectations.

No wonder we have such messes with anger.

If I expect certain behavior that I don't get, I can become angry. Or I can change my expectations.

38

To Be Truly Strong

"I don't forgive; I just get even." I remember hearing that statement in a movie and people cheered.

It's clever.

It's also sad.

The movie, I remember, was about revenge. The bad people did something to the hero, and he planned to hurt them worse than they had injured him. The message is that he was strong and powerful and, consequently, he wouldn't forgive.

I don't believe in injustice, and I don't think we ought to forget the concept of justice when people do terrible things to us. Because I believe in fairness and integrity, I also say that people need to face their own wrongdoings.

Few of us get caught in life-and-death situations or those times where retaliation seems to be the only way to right the wrongs. Gandhi and Martin Luther King Jr. advocated peaceful nonviolence. They passively stood up to societal evils and were willing to go to jail for breaking laws they considered unjust.

With most of us, however, the injustices around us are the words of unkindness, the preferential treatment someone received, the lies someone told about us, or our hard work for which someone else received credit.

Most of us like to think of ourselves as strong. Stalwart. That we stand up for the right. I feel the same way.

But there's one quality that we need to be truly strong. There is one thing we can do. It's not advice for cowards or weaklings; it's advice for those who understand life.

Here it is: *we forgive.* It may not be easy, and we may have to struggle to release our hurts. We have to get past thinking they deserve any punishment we can think of heaping on those who injure us.

But as long as we withhold forgiveness from others, we're the losers; we're the weaklings. It takes real strength of character to say to someone, "I forgive you," and truly mean it. It's even more courageous when they obviously intended to do us harm.

It takes real strength of character
to say to someone, "I forgive you,"
and truly mean it.

I'm reminded of a story in the book of Genesis. At age seventeen, Joseph's brothers are jealous (with some justification), and hate him (for which there is no justification). They sell him to traders, who take him to Egypt and sell him again. Joseph's saga is the longest account in the book of Genesis; we read of one grave injustice to him after another.

Joseph eventually becomes the second most important person in Egypt, subject only to King Pharaoh. He saves those who later become the nation of Israel.

Despite the evil done to him, Joseph maintains his integrity; we have no record of bitterness or anger toward his ten brothers. In the final chapter of the book of Genesis, their father, Jacob, dies. The brothers assume that, with their father's passing, Joseph will avenge himself. That's probably what they would do, and they assume he thinks the same way. They go to their brother, beg him to forgive them, and cry out finally, "We are your slaves!"[6]

But Joseph is stronger than they are. "Don't be afraid of me. Am I God, that I can punish you? You intended to harm me, but God intended it all for good. He brought me to this position so I could save the lives of many people. No, don't be afraid."[7]

Joseph forgives his brothers even though he faced death, endured years of unjust servitude, and was wrongly accused of a crime. That's a strong person. That's someone whose actions also say, "I'm strong enough to forgive."

Even though I'm weak in many ways,
I want to be strong
and forgive those who have hurt me.

39

Only the Strong

THE OTHER DAY I RECEIVED an e-mail from a friend. He had asked me for the address of another friend, and I pasted it from my database. Two days later my friend wrote, *The e-mail address you gave me was wrong. Please send me the correct one.* He enclosed the e-mail he had sent. He had inadvertently corrupted the address, so naturally it came back.

Instead of sending the address again, I simply forwarded his e-mail. My friend received it, replied to him, and everything was fine.

Except (this is trivial, but it says something about my friend) he was wrong and he didn't admit that it was his mistake. He blamed me. He could have sent me a simple message to say the e-mail was returned, with no blame attached. But he was unwilling to admit his mistake.

I've known that friend for nearly twenty years, and it's a trait I'd noticed before in him. I'm not writing this to condemn him. Instead, I want to propose an antidote.

I want to share one simple, empowering statement. It doesn't have to be in these exact words as long as it carries the message: "I was mistaken." We can make it lighter with a simple "Mea culpa." I often hear "My bad" today. They all work—when we mean them.

Yet I've discovered some people can't use such simple statements. "It makes me feel weak," one man said when I tried to push him.

I countered with "Only the strong can say 'I was wrong' or 'I'm sorry.'" I probably read that somewhere, but it fit the situation.

All of us make mistakes and errors of judgment; that's part of being alive. But the stalwart and the successful are those who take responsibility for their own failures. And sometimes being responsible is the beginning of solving a serious problem.

"I made a mistake." Four words. Or try "I was wrong." That's only three.

It's not a natural reaction to admit we were in error, but it's a great skill to practice. The more frequently we can admit our mistakes, the more empowered we are. Perhaps that sounds contradictory.

> "I made a mistake."
> Four words.
> Or try "I was wrong."
> That's only three.

To admit we failed, that we took the wrong attitude, that we made a mistake in judgment—that's empowering. Liberating. To face our failures eliminates a tremendous expenditure of energy to hide our shortcomings, to point the blame at others, or to deny knowledge.

I've noticed this principle in national and international news. When celebrities get into any kind of trouble, their first reaction is usually to deny the accusation. But if the allegations are true, the truth often comes out: drug use by sports stars, sexual misconduct by a leading cleric, or fraud by a tycoon on Wall Street.

The few (and there have been only a few) who stood up and

said, "I did it. I was wrong, and I'm sorry," won our admiration. We forgave them or overlooked their wrongdoing. But the others, who eventually must make similar statements because the evidence is there to convict them, have little effect on us. They lied to us, and they tried to deceive us. We lose respect for them—respect they can't easily earn back.

Those who admit their failures immediately may not move back into the places of prominence, but we admire them. And we empower them so they can hold up their heads in public.

Perhaps it's obvious what the answer is. If it is, here's my question: Why don't we do it?

I'll go back to a statement I made above:

Only the strong can say "I was wrong" or "I'm sorry."

40

Forgiveness Isn't Absolution

NOT LONG AGO I READ an interesting statement on a blog. The person wrote about knowing she had to forgive her parents for the way they had mistreated her, although she didn't go into any detail about the issues. She went on to speak of her resentment and her resistance to forgiving them. She stated that if she forgave them, it would be as if she were giving them a free pass for all the hurt they caused.

Those were insightful words, and I pondered them off and on for a couple of days. I did appreciate that she was aware that forgiving or not forgiving was her issue, not theirs.

By forgiving them (which she did after a long, intense struggle), she no longer had to carry painful memories inside her head and heart. For a long time she had held on to her unwillingness to forgive them, as if it hurt them.

"They'd both been dead for more than five years, and I still held on," she said. "One day I asked myself, 'How am I hurting them?' That's when I decided I had to forgive—not for them, but for me."

She made two more important points:

First, when we forgive, we don't absolve others from what they did.

Second, if we hold on and refuse to forgive, we make ourselves prisoners of our own hatred and pain. In some ways that feels doubly painful. Not only do people hurt us, but if we hold on and refuse to let go, we are empowering their past actions to continue to hurt us in the present.

To genuinely forgive others sets *us* free. We can refuse to hold on to our pain and open the prison doors of pain and suffering through forgiveness.

To genuinely forgive others sets *us* free.

Granted that the woman's story was extremely dramatic and most of our hurts don't hit us that strongly. People take advantage of us, they betray our confidence, they lie to us, or they lie about us. Most of our hurts from others come in small doses. It may not seem that way at the time, but as we gain perspective, we know that's true.

But small or large, it hurts. It's as if we've developed an infection. We can take drastic action, or we can allow that infection to grow inside us and upset our entire system. We can let it poison us so that even the mention of that person's name brings more pain and deeper infection.

Using a different metaphor, we can choose to walk out of the cell of emotional darkness and into wonderful light.

Forgiveness admits that we have felt the hurt. We haven't ignored it or run from it. If we deny we're injured, we're only allowing the infection to spread. Once we're tired of the emotional ups and downs of fighting the enemies, who probably don't even know they're enemies (or don't care if they do know), we begin to take action.

We do it selfishly—we forgive for ourselves and because we want a better life. And as the woman concluded on her blog, it's not absolving others to forgive them. It means we admit what they've done, even if they never acknowledge any wrongdoing or being the source of pain.

Our forgiving others shows how much we value God's forgiving us. As we recognize our own failures and how little we deserve divine pardon—which we call grace—we're able to forgive.

To forgive isn't to absolve them but to absolve ourselves from bitterness and pain.

I don't forgive to absolve others.
I forgive to set myself free.

41

A New Lesson in Forgiveness

I'VE HAD TO FORGIVE many people over many, many years of life. To forgive others is built into every religion and each ethical culture. We have to learn to move beyond the slights or direct assaults on us.

Some forgive more easily than others do, and we all forgive more readily in certain circumstances.

I learned an invaluable lesson about forgiveness many years ago. I attended a community business meeting, and a man whose name I can only remember as Mac McMillan was under fire. A number of people in the community were upset over the way he handled things. I knew little about the situation but went because I had a brief presentation on a different topic.

My wife was ill so I took our son, John Mark, with me. He was about eight months old and had been fussy all day. For the first part of the meeting and while I made my presentation, he slept in his bassinette. About ten minutes after I sat down, John Mark began to whimper. I was afraid he would cry loudly so I picked him up and took him out into the foyer.

Just then a woman came out of the restroom. I knew her slightly, and she came over and we talked about babies. Neither of us said anything about what was going on inside.

At that moment, Mac stepped out and drank from the water cooler. He turned and stared at her and then at me. She immediately went back inside.

"That's the way you operate, is it?" he yelled at me. "You can't raise objections or ask questions, but you come out here to get people lined up against me?" He went on a tirade, giving me no chance to reply.

John Mark started to cry—probably because of the noise. I tried to explain to Mac that we hadn't discussed anything that involved him. He walked away, and just before he went back into the meeting through another door, he yelled something. I couldn't hear what it was.

John Mark cried louder, so I decided to take him home. But I kept thinking about what Mac said. I was innocent, and he hadn't been courteous enough to give me the chance to explain.

I withdrew from that community group and never saw Mac again. But I didn't forget him. He was wrong, and I was right. It made me angry that I didn't have a chance to straighten him out.

I'm not sure how long I held on to my anger and hurt. I hadn't known Mac well, but I had certainly not been against him. I kept trying to figure out ways to explain, to make him see that he had been mistaken.

We moved shortly after that so Mac was out of my life, but the memory and the anger were still there. One day I realized something: *I didn't want to forgive.* I only wanted to prove him wrong. I wanted to see him again and tell him what a stupid, angry man he was.

> ## It made me angry that I didn't have a chance to straighten him out.

As long as I felt a compulsion to show him the truth, tell him how badly he had behaved, or prove that he had misjudged me, I couldn't let it go. Once I didn't need to be right, I was able to forgive him.

The principle works that way in all kinds of situations. So often in disputes with others I've needed to be right or in the right. Holding on has proven a strange sort of comfort. I can tell myself how awful the other person is and, by extension, how good and noble I am.

Once I was able to ignore what Mac had done and focus on my attitude, I was able to let go. Simple? Yes, but as long as I needed to be innocent, right, or righteous, I couldn't let go.

Once I could put aside my self-righteousness—and that's what it was—I could say, "I forgive Mac." I also said, "I forgive myself for holding on to this."

When I no longer need to be right, I'm able to forgive.

42

Forgiving Ourselves

"I'VE MESSED UP."

"I've failed."

"I haven't lived up to my own ideals."

Most of us have said things like that to ourselves many times. Who of us ever does it right every time? That's not to encourage failure, but to help us accept it as part of life.

One of the things about life that doesn't make sense to me is that often I know exactly the right thing to do. I tell myself that I'll do it and then I don't. I work against what I know is right.

Perhaps it's because I'm weak willed, or perhaps it's because my will to do what I want is too strong.

More often, my problem is simpler. I make mistakes. Some may choose to say, "I fail," or "I sin," or "I do something stupid"—and all are true. In time I move beyond those events. But the place where I have trouble is in forgiving myself.

For example, certain people upset me. I'm aware they touch sensitive parts of my psyche so I'm sucked into a confrontation. I don't always verbalize my feelings, but I'm aware of them. I don't yell, "You're a jerk!" and I don't try to retaliate.

After I'm calm and away from their presence, I replay the incident. To forgive those individuals for being rude or insensitive doesn't usually present a big problem. The real struggle is to forgive myself.

Here's the reason: I know better. I've mouthed off. I've said or thought something inappropriate. Just because the other person is rude doesn't entitle me to respond the same way. If I do something that I consider unethical or unkind and figure it out later, I excuse myself by saying, "I didn't realize what I'd done."

But that's not the usual problem.

I know better.

That's the sore spot. If I yelled in shocked anger or became aware only later of my bad behavior, I wouldn't be so bothered. But I know what I'm doing. I know exactly what I am doing at the very moment I do it.

I once tried to explain this to a corpulent friend as we sat at a potluck dinner at church. He couldn't seem to grasp what I was saying. I stopped trying to explain and said, "That's the third dessert you've eaten."

"I know, but I can't resist—"

That's when I laughed.

Marv understood. "You're right. I know better, but I just can't leave the sweet stuff alone."

Marv's solution was to gain more weight and continue to feel guilty every time he overate—which was at least once daily.

Weight isn't a problem for me, but I struggle with some annoying habits (I like that better than calling them *little sins*). I know better, but I do them anyway.

Two things have helped me in my battle.

One is that I read the words of a very learned man—probably the most famous living Christian of the first century...the apostle Paul. He wrote to people in Rome: "I want to do what is good, but I don't. I don't want to do what is wrong, but I do it anyway."[8] That helped me realize that even the most holy of people still fail. I don't want that to be an excuse, but it reminds me that none of us reaches perfection.

> I struggle with some annoying habits (I like that better than calling them *little sins*). I know better, but I do them anyway.

Second, a friend named Bob Ramey once listened to my self-flagellation and said, "If I were the person who kept doing something wrong to you and each time asked you to forgive me, would you do that?"

"Certainly."

"Be as kind to Cec as you would be to me."

That sounds simplistic and perhaps it is, but that single statement changed my thinking. If I could see Cec Murphey as another human being and was aware of his failure—even though he knew better—I would forgive him.

I've had to learn to become as compassionate toward myself as I am toward others. Bob taught me a powerful lesson.

Because I've learned to forgive others,
I can learn to forgive myself.

43

Needing
My Enemies

HIS WORDS STUNNED ME. During a seminar break, three of us talked about the negative people in our lives and how difficult they made things for us. Two told stories about cantankerous individuals with whom they had dealt.

I was ready to tell about a particularly offensive person when a fourth man, a stranger whose name I never learned, overheard us and said, "You need your enemies, you know."

"And why would I need my enemies?" I asked. "Why would I need individuals to make my life worse?"

"You figure it out," he said and walked away.

One of my friends mentioned how rude the stranger was and that moved the conversation in a different direction. But on the way home, I thought about the comment the intruder made.

Although that happened weeks ago, as I continued to ponder his statement, I've decided that he's right. I need those negative, hateful, harsh, mean-spirited people in my life.

I don't like what they say, and sometimes I'm offended. A few times I've gotten angry over things they've done. I've resented them and wanted to retaliate by telling them how despicable and insensitive they are. (I haven't usually done those things, but I've thought about them.)

And yet I need those enemies. I need them because my friends affirm the good things in my life. They appreciate me and encourage me. Sometimes they say negative things about me, but I can usually accept the comments. Because they love me, they coat the most critical remarks with warm, loving words.

Enemies often do us a favor.... They push us to admit our imperfections and shortcomings.

But not my enemies. They don't usually try to soften their words but blare them out. I'm not sure if they intend to hurt me (possibly), or if they say it for what they consider my own good (another possibility), or maybe they're just negative people (could be).

Here's something I've learned—and it hasn't been easy—those enemies often do us a favor. Think about the coworker who's always in your face trying to tell you how to do something better. What about the one neighbor who complains frequently about you not mowing your lawn? What about those obnoxious individuals who tell you that you talk too much, don't talk enough, speak too loudly, or your voice is too soft?

They often lash out and move on. Our immediate instinct, of course, is that they're wrong. Often they are. If we're wise, however, we listen to what they say. Sometimes they see parts of us that we haven't seen or don't want to face. They push us to admit our imperfections and shortcomings.

On a recent Sunday morning in our church, one of our pastors preached from the Sermon on the Mount—Jesus' instructions to followers found in Matthew, chapters five through seven.

The part that struck me was "You have heard the law that says, 'Love your neighbor,' and hate your enemy. But I say, love your enemies!"[9]

"If you don't like the word *enemy*," the preacher suggested, "use *opponent*," which was a good synonym. (After all, we were in church, and supposedly we don't hate anyone.)

As a result of that message, I've spent time giving thanks to God for my enemies—whom I define as those who don't like me or who criticize me. Too often they were right in their criticism but wrong in their delivery.

Those people who belittle me or point out such things enable me to see a side of myself that I wouldn't choose to admit. They make me a better person because I have to think about what they say. Even when they're totally wrong, they push me to examine myself, my attitudes, and my motives.

I need my opponents.
They often speak the truths that my friends won't.

44

Guarding
Our Secrets

As I walked away from a group of fifteen men who met twice monthly to share the pain of their childhood sexual and physical abuse, I pondered what they told me.

The one thing that struck me (though no one said it in these words) was: nothing is as lonely as guarding our own secrets. As long as I have something hidden and undisclosed, I find myself constantly protecting it. And I refer to those things of which we feel ashamed or embarrassed, around which we spend immense energy erecting protective walls to keep out intruders.

We don't want others to know our deepest thoughts and feelings, and certainly not the unacceptable parts of our past. *If others know those things, they won't like us or they might reject us,* we think.

I know this from experience. I kept something hidden because I didn't feel I could tell anyone. By most standards, that undisclosed information probably wasn't significant—and I realize it only in retrospect. But my secret troubled me, and I didn't want anyone to know about it.

One day I decided that I'd held the secret long enough and that I could finally reveal the details to my friend David Morgan.

David and I meet almost every week for an hour or possibly two. Our one agenda is to open up to each other. We don't talk about sports, jobs, or politics—unless they directly influence something going on inside us.

> One day I decided that I'd held the secret long enough.

I told him it was a secret that lay heavily on my soul. I dropped my head because I was too ashamed to look into his eyes. The confession came out, and I stopped.

David said nothing.

I looked at him.

"And?" he asked.

"That's it."

"Oh."

His one-word response shocked me. "Is that all you're going to say?"

David shrugged. "What do you want me to say?" And he laughed.

I laughed too. My friend had heard my deepest held, shameful secret and in his way, he was saying, "Okay, so what? Do you think that makes any difference in the way I feel about you?" His non-judgmental response freed me from my shame.

I'm sorry I had the terrible experience, but the freedom was marvelous. In theory I had known for a long time that I could tell David anything and he wouldn't condemn me. And I did talk about everything...except *THAT*.

After I took the risk, I knew I had done the right thing. My long-hidden deed was no longer something underground and threatening. It was as if a large growth had been excised. I was free.

I don't advocate blabbing our inmost thoughts and actions indiscriminately, but if I never tell anyone, I'm desperately lonely or I'm afraid. My past holds me back from fully enjoying my future.

I used to think when I spoke to those I would call good friends, *You don't really know me because you don't know the deepest, most shameful part of me.*

And the secret (or many secrets) becomes an estrangement. Not always big, but enough that it was as if I held out a sign: DANGER. GO NO FURTHER.

For me, holding on to a shameful act was a strange phenomenon. As a Christian man, I believe in confession. I had confessed that deed to God and asked for forgiveness. I didn't question whether I was forgiven; I assumed I was.

But I still carried an appalling shameful reminder. I finally figured out that I also needed a flesh-and-blood person—someone whom I could look in the face and say, "I want to tell you..."

When another human being hears, understands, and accepts me, I truly know I'm forgiven—and set free.

Nothing is as lonely as guarding my secrets. Nothing else separates me more from other human beings than hiding part of myself.

45

The People We Remember

WHEN LIFE ISN'T MAKING MUCH SENSE and everything seems to throw us into a downward spiral, I have one significant thing to say: be careful whom you tell about your situations. This isn't about whom to trust; it's about the *effect* the conversation will have on you.

One time after Sunday school, Tim Fenbert and I spoke for perhaps five minutes. I don't remember anything specific he said. He didn't give me any words of encouragement or add to my knowledge, but I left feeling uplifted just from being with him.

Later in the day Dan and I talked for almost an hour. I could write a two-page summary of our conversation. After we parted, however, I realized I left with about the same emotional temperature with which we began. That's not a complaint, yet it's typical of many encounters.

The next day, I had coffee with Rick. Most of the talk was about how badly he had been treated at work. He didn't get the promotion he had expected and his job-approval rating was "good, but not excellent." He was resentful.

When I went to bed that night, I reviewed the three conversations. Rick was the worst meeting I'd had in weeks. The time with Dan was all right—not particularly special—and I learned a few things.

The time with Tim, however, was the shortest dialogue of the three. I don't remember what Tim said; I can't forget how he made me feel.

That's the point I want to make. When life is a mess or doesn't make sense, seek out men or women like Tim Fenbert.

> I don't remember what Tim said; I can't forget how he made me feel.

Before long, I dismissed Don and Rick and focused on Tim. I still felt a quiet glow inside when I thought about being with him. He focuses on my face when he talks, and I feel he's trying to stare into my heart.

And Tim isn't the only such person in my life. As I waited for my mind to drift into sleep I thought of others in my life who are like Tim.

I meet with Deidre Knight, my literary agent, for lunch a few times a year. What we discuss isn't nearly as important as my emotional level by the time she hugs me good-bye. I'm pumped. Excited. Just being with Deidre and exchanging ideas excites me.

She's represented me since 1997, and I can't think of a single time we've met in person when I didn't leave feeling uplifted and encouraged. Even when she told me about editors rejecting my manuscripts, her presence lessened the impact of the bad news.

The other example involves a Sunday school teacher, Marie Garbie. When I was about ten years old, I was in her class for only a few months. She wasn't a particularly good teacher. But years later, when I was open enough to turn to God, I wanted to share my conversion experience with her.

I smile as I think of the reason. I don't remember anything she taught, but she made me feel that I was the best kid who had ever attended her class (and she taught many, many years). It wasn't that she said those words, or at least I don't think so, but that's how I felt.

The people like Tim, Deidre, and my one-time childhood Sunday school teacher are the kind of people with whom I want to invest my life. I don't want to ignore the hurting and the pain-filled. And there are times I need to be with them to lift them up. But when I'm down and life is messy, those special people I've mentioned are the ones I need to enjoy.

Why should I be around those who will depress me or discourage me? I want to be with those who, just by their presence, make me feel loved and want to succeed.

I spend time with those who make me feel better;
I avoid those who discourage me or pull me down.
I strive to be a person whom others remember
because of the way I make them feel.

46

What We Can Do

A LARGE CORPORATION bought the company for which Eric worked. They classified him as "redundant," and he became jobless.

Two months later Eric asked me to meet with him for coffee because he felt he had to talk to someone. "When I try to open up to my wife, she worries or cries," he said

Three or four times he repeated, "I'll never find another job as good as that one." I didn't know how to respond. Eric finally ran out of words and looked at me. His eyes seemed to beg for help. "Tell me anything," he said. "Any suggestion. I'm open."

I mentioned other jobs in his general field, but they weren't quite the same as his. He always had a reason why none of them would be right for him.

"I don't have the education," he said about two of the possibilities. "I don't have the skills for that," he said about another.

"Have you thought about going back to college to upgrade your skills or train for something new?"

"I couldn't do that." He explained all his financial problems—a mortgage and car payments—the usual list.

"Have you talked to some of your friends? Asked them if they know anything you could look into?"

He shook his head. "Yeah, but none of them seem to want to help me."

No wonder. He had a negative response for every suggestion made. What I learned from Eric (and have observed in others as well) is that such people are fairly clear on what they *can't* do; however, they don't seem to be able to think about what they *can* do.

They give reasons they can't succeed or explain why life has failed them or others jump ahead of them in line. It's difficult to help the Erics of the world.

But here's something I've thought of hundreds of times. When I was a teenager, I worked for a man who owned several businesses. One of them was a donut shop. Above his donut machine he had posted a poem, which I memorized:

As you wander on through life, brother,
Whatever be your goal,
Keep your eye upon the donut,
And not upon the hole.

That day as I spoke with Eric I thought of that badly written but insightful doggerel. Eric was so focused on the hole in his life he seemed unable to grasp anything else. He couldn't focus on possibilities or on trying something new and daring.

For many of us, that's a stage we have to go through. Because we're down, we can think only of what we can't do, we don't want to do, or we're unable to do. We need to get past that and ask ourselves, "What can I do?"

That's when we take our eyes off the empty place. But if we continue to stare at what's *not* there, it becomes like the infamous black hole that seems to have no end. We figure out what we've lost, perhaps what we can never have again, or moan that life is passing us by.

Eric still doesn't have steady employment after almost three years. I think he's taken up residence inside the black hole and can't look beyond what he can't do.

Life isn't always fun, and often things don't make sense. But we can stop staring at the emptiness of life and focus on what might fill us with contentment, maybe even joy.

There are many things I can't do.
But more important is what I can do.

47

Aiming and Settling

OUR SON, JOHN MARK, was in boarding school in Africa. It was parents' day and one of the highlights was the hundred-yard dash. Our son was excited because he had signed up to participate. "I'm going to win," he said at least twice. His smile made me realize he believed his words.

The race began and he plunged ahead, gaze fixed on the finish line. His face beamed and he surged forward, determination and assurance of victory evident.

Our son came in last.

John Mark was the only first-grade boy, and the other nine boys were fourth through eighth graders. He hadn't had a chance to win, but he didn't know that. He aimed to win and had to settle for last place.

He cried and I hugged him, speaking meaningless words about life not being fair. While I felt his terrible disappointment, there was nothing I could do to change the results.

And that's the way it is with many of us. We face odds we don't know about. We're naïve enough to think that we can beat whatever obstacles we face. And sometimes we do win.

But not always. And for some, not often.

I suppose most of us live between those two words of aiming and settling. To aim means to dream, to envision success, to yearn for the top rung on the ladder. We're sure of what we would like to achieve, and if we continue to work diligently, we can reach our goals.

> Most of us live between those two words of aiming and settling.

But too often we don't reach the top. We feel as if something is almost within our grasp, but we can't stretch our hands quite far enough to grasp it. So we settle for what we have. At times we do it joyfully, but on most occasions, we do it reluctantly. We might console ourselves with "I tried."

No one lives that charmed life of succeeding at everything. And it hurts us to realize that people less talented, less qualified, and less ambitious pass us by or achieve the very things we want. "It seems unfair" is one thing we say. Or we can rail against stupid bosses who can't see our potential.

But that's how life is, and there are occasions when all of us need to learn to settle. By that I mean to accept life the way it is. We give it our best, and we don't make the grade or get what we seek. We have failed at one thing we wanted badly. But as the saying goes, "We've failed at one thing, but we haven't failed at life." That is, unless we just quit.

Through the years I've met many people who can't seem to win and can't settle for what they have. They can usually tell me that everything is against them, that the "good ol' boy" network still controls the results, or that they refuse to join the clique and compromise their ethical principles.

For most of us, however, life becomes a matter of aiming for the best and settling for what we achieve. My friend Jeff Adams says it this way: "Aim for perfection; settle for excellence."

> No one lives that charmed life of succeeding at everything.

That's how I feel. As a writer, every time I agree to write a manuscript, I yearn for it to be flawless. I want it to be so good that an editor can't make one correction.

I've never been able to turn in a perfect manuscript. My editors have always found something to change. For me to turn in a perfect manuscript won't happen. That doesn't stop me from trying or from yearning to be perfect, but it does mean I have to settle for excellence. (And "excellence" means producing the best work I'm capable of turning out.)

I know that, but I still follow Jeff's advice. I aim for the top and settle for almost.

Despite that, and no matter how hard we work, at some point we get trounced. Even if we think it's the best, the other person may despise our work or ridicule it.

Once our second daughter, Cecile, received a grade of D in social studies. She is an artist and, typical of that personality, she wasn't a high academic achiever. It was even harder for her, I think, because her older sister always brought in excellent grades. Tears filled Cecile's eyes when she showed me her report card.

I hugged her. "Did you do your best?" I asked. That's what I asked of all three of our children.

She nodded. "I did, Daddy, I did."

"That's all that counts," I said. (She worked hard and pulled her final grade up to C for the year.)

I had said those words to her, but a few times I've had to remember them and say to myself: "I did my best." I had aimed high. I missed, but I tried.

No matter how hard I try or how high I aim, I don't always achieve my goals, but I can learn to settle for doing my best.

48

Reaching for Power

MOST OF US LIKE THE WORD *POWER*, especially if it refers to something we can control. If we can be in charge, we feel better. We may not always like the responsibility or accountability of standing on the top rung of the ladder, but doesn't it feel wonderful to think of ourselves as the best at something?

And maybe that's one of the problems. We want power; we want to take charge and stand at the crest of the hill.

In reality, few of us reach that summit. Even if we do, it's not for long. A few years ago, my friend Jud Knight pointed out the prominence of top-grossing movie stars. "They typically stay at the apex for about three years," he said, "and by the fourth year someone else eclipses them."

I thought it was insightful, whether it's literally three years or seven. No matter how high we climb, we can't maintain our position at the top. There's always someone (or many) trying to wrest the power from us.

If that's a general truth, maybe we need to look at power in a different light, and in a way that goes contrary to Western thinking. What if we let the power control us?

I'll try it another way. Alcoholics Anonymous and other mutual-help groups have 12-step programs. The first step in such groups begins with, "We admitted we were powerless over alcohol" (or drugs or sex), followed by admitting that they believe a "power greater than ourselves could restore us to sanity." The third step says they decided "to turn our will and our lives over to the care of God as we understand Him."

It's quite amazing how much God language there is in the 12 Steps. They're also careful to speak of God as individuals understand the term. Most AA members I know refer to a "Higher Power," and a few speak of the Creator.

Regardless of the term, their perceptions resonate with me because they imply that all of them hit the bottom of a big hole and couldn't pull themselves out. But they lifted their arm, and someone, a power stronger than themselves, pulled them out.

And it doesn't have to be alcohol, prescription drugs, or sexual addiction to make us cry out for a stronger power outside ourselves. When we're so low the only direction we can look is up, we reach for the power beyond ourselves.

Although I came from an alcoholic family, I've never been addicted. But I did come to the place of intense need. My story is simple. At age sixteen I learned the word *agnostic* and felt it described me. I didn't know if there was a God and didn't care.

> When we're so low the only direction we can look is up, we reach for the power beyond ourselves.

At age twenty-one, however, I faced life and asked, "Is this all there is?" I had been dumped by a woman with whom I had expected to spend the rest of my life, and I was sensible enough to know that I wasn't the first man to whom that had happened. But the trauma of that event forced me to ask, "Is this all there is to life? Birth, death, and ups and downs in between?"

If that's all there is, I wondered, *is life worth the effort?* That may sound like depression or despair, but it was neither. For me, that was the moment (actually a period of months) when I admitted that there must be something more in life than what I had experienced.

After eight or nine months of thinking, talking to others, and especially a time of reading, I began a new phase of my life. I became a serious Christian. That's when I began to attach words like *meaning* and *purpose* to my life.

And what does that have to do with power? In my darkest moments, I realized, probably to a lesser degree than many addicts, that I was powerless. I had skills and gifts; I worked hard and knew I could probably succeed in whatever field I entered. But that wasn't enough.

"So what? Does that mean anything?" I asked. "Is there no purpose to my life?"

I knew all the right things to do, and I knew I couldn't force meaning into my world. I needed something beyond myself. Again, I'm not the first (or the last) to figure out that reality. When we have something bigger than ourselves, we have meaning.

I also have a purpose. I don't know everything about why I'm here on earth at just this time, but I'm aware of at least three reasons.

1. I'm here to enjoy my world.
2. I'm here to grow as an individual.
3. I'm here to reach out and wrap my arms around other people.

I choose to serve a God who embodies endless love and enduring compassion. When I fail (and I'm quite good at being unable to live up to my highest ideals), I have a place of absolution. I confess to God. Because, as a serious Christian, I'm convinced that God forgives me when I confess, and I am empowered to get back into life and to try again.

I don't possess a higher power, but I'm connected to a Higher Power.

49

Defining Success

HIS QUESTION SHOCKED ME, perhaps because I hadn't thought about it before. He said, "You're successful. How did you get that way?"

"I suppose I am successful—I simply hadn't considered whether I was or wasn't."

When I spoke those words, he laughed. "That's because you are. If you weren't successful, you'd probably worry about it every day."

Maybe.

Or perhaps it's something the want-to-be-successful-people-who-aren't feel they have to ask. The man who questioned me had qualities that breed accomplishment. The son of a wealthy entrepreneur, he was bright, well-educated, and articulate. Being tall and handsome didn't hurt. But somehow he self-sabotaged time and again.

I wasn't able to give him an answer for two reasons.

First, I don't know how to define success. It's like the question, "How much money would you need to be rich?" It's an individual response.

For one person, to raise well-adjusted, contented children would be a standard of significant achievement. To another, fame or high-level accomplishment in a chosen field would do it.

Second, I don't know the right steps to take to be successful. Years ago I taught an adult Sunday school class and a woman named Tracy answered a different question with these words: "Do the next right thing."

That may sound simplistic, but that statement became my favorite mantra when I wasn't sure about a direction. I took the next *right* step. I didn't know where I was going, but if I went forward, always doing what I knew was right and not giving up, it was the correct step.

"Do the next right thing."

Here's what I've finally figured out. People may deny it, but they know—or at least sense—when they're taking a wrong step. On some level they know even if they ignore their inner wisdom and stumble onto the road of expediency.

An old proverb says it well: "If we are facing in the right direction, all we have to do is keep on walking."

Am I successful? My answer is: yes, in some things.

However, that isn't the kind of question I ask myself. I focus on being the best Cec Murphey I know how to be. The more I look at myself and measure myself by what I know is right, the more my life makes sense. When I allow someone else's standard to become the way to measure myself, I see myself as less accomplished.

When I went to grad school, I studied in the field of education. We had a required course called Tests and Measurements. Instead of being able to use charts for the standard IQ tests, we had to take the test results and compute the information and arrive at the correct IQ scores.

That was the most challenging course I had in my entire academic career. I received a grade of D—the first and only D I ever received. But for that course, a D was a pass, and the grade didn't appear on our transcripts.

Was I successful in that course? By my standards, absolutely yes, because I didn't fail the course. Not having to retake the class was my measurement. Although some of my friends scored grades of A and B, I didn't compare myself with them. If I had, I would have felt like a failure. I'm not good with numbers, and I hate to balance a checkbook.

Instead of focusing on my lack of math skills, my definition of success comes from within. When I choose the higher path in any situation—the path of integrity—I'm successful, even though the results may not be acceptable to someone else. Besides, those to whom I might compare myself probably don't notice or care whether I achieve or fail.

Recently a friend said, "There are two simple principles to success. First, figure out what interests you and *what* you do well. Second, once you've discovered it, throw all your ability and energy into it."

He was right: simple. Not always easy, but definitely simple.

No one else can define my success.
I get to choose my own definition.

50

Our Greatest Strengths

WHEN I WAS IN COLLEGE, one of my professors said, "Your greatest strength is also your greatest weakness." That sounded good, but he didn't elaborate on his statement.

If I understand what he meant, I agree.

For example, the Africans named me *Haraka*, which means "quick" or "fast." I smiled when I first heard that sobriquet, because it was an apt description. When I was in high school, my last class before lunch always seemed to be at the farthest end of the building from the cafeteria. But I moved quickly enough (without running) that not more than a dozen students reached the line before I did.

The assistant principal, Mr. Hempstead, used to shake his head and call out, "There goes speedy Murphey." So when the Africans called me Haraka, it was because they had observed the same behavior.

I like that quality. I get more miles out of my day than some people.

But there is the inevitable downside. Sometimes I bypass the details. There is an old saying about pausing to smell the roses, and I didn't always take time to do that. I missed out on small things that would have made my life more meaningful.

When I was a pastor, a few people said, "You were so busy, I felt you didn't have time for me."

That's a comment we rapid-moving people receive regularly. Those words hurt, and they weren't true, but I understood what they meant. I seemed always on the fast track, and I didn't slow down. I could have defended myself, but there was enough truth in what they said to silence me.

My college professor was right: my strength was also my weakness. I've shared a strong-weak feature, and we all have them. The late Maureen Hamilton was a compassionate listener, and people opened up to her. The downside is that she stayed and stayed and stayed, seemingly unable to stop listening. The complaint I heard was, "She just didn't seem to know when to go home."

> I like that quality. I get more miles out of my day than some people. But there is the inevitable downside. Sometimes I bypass the details.

Perhaps one reason we have many messes in our lives is that we stress our strengths—and they're natural for us—and deny the negative sides of our personalities. It's difficult to pay attention to the weaker half, but part of bringing peace and harmony into our lives involves learning to hold back on the natural tendencies and to cultivate the "lesser" side of our lives.

I like the way my friend Woody McKay says it: "God, give me the strength to deal with my weaknesses."

I value my strengths
while I remain aware they are also my weaknesses.

51

Ignoring Success

"HOW CAN I BECOME SUCCESSFUL?" It's almost laughable when I hear that question from someone who's twenty years old. That's when it seems as if the individuals mean, "How can I start at the top instead of having to go through all the painful steps to get there?"

Or perhaps they're trying to say they want guidance to move in the right direction toward success as a lawyer, an accountant, teacher, or (as most of those who come to me) as a writer.

"It's the wrong question to ask," is my usual answer. "You're putting your energies and attention in the wrong place. Ignore success."

That usually raises serious questions. They remind me that success is important and of how they want to be significant. I often hear, "I want to make a difference." Many of the want-to-be writers insist they have a story that will dazzle millions and be made into a box-office smashing film. Or they have a message that people need to read to improve their lives (or enable them to live longer or healthier or happier).

I understand their desire to reach the top of the mountain, and I'm not opposed to success. By most standards I'm successful, but that is not and has not been my intention. As a writer, here's my way of saying it: I committed myself to learn and to continue to learn. I didn't pray for success (and didn't really expect it).

One time—and only once—I prayed for a book to sell one hundred thousand copies—and I did that only because a friend urged me to do so. He wanted me to pray for a million copies, but that number was too far out of my range.

I laugh now because that book sold fewer than four thousand copies. I didn't pray that way again. Instead, I focused on doing my best and continuing to improve.

Focus on whatever your heart leads you to do....
Concentrate on doing what you can
to achieve your goal.

Success has come for me, but not because of a focus on fame or achievement. If we concentrate on those targets, we'll be disappointed. Haven't we all heard that the journey is more important than the destination? I believe that.

So I'm successful. That means I sell books. I have enough income from writing that I live comfortably. But more significant to me is that I love what I do. Each morning it's a joy to me to sit in front of my computer screen and feel the words flow from my mind to my fingers to the screen.

Here's my advice: follow your dreams. Focus on whatever your heart leads you to do. What do you want to accomplish? Concentrate on doing what you can to achieve your goal.

Too often we define success as achievement, and that's supposed to be the pinnacle of bliss. When I hear people talk that way, I remember reading the death notice many years ago of the then-famous actor George Sanders. He won an academy award, was a top movie star for at least three decades, and had four wives. He committed suicide, and his note read, "Life is a bore."

Fame, admiration, and money obviously didn't satisfy Sanders.

And they won't satisfy any of us as long as we focus on the illusive success.

However, if we follow our God-given passion, we may not know where it will lead, but we'll become "successful" because we've followed our desires. That's what brings happiness, isn't it?

I ignore success;
I pursue my dreams.

52

The Sweet Spot

WE HEAR THE TERM *sweet spot* used often. It's originally a sports term, and I believe it came from baseball. The sweet spot is the location on the bat that connects with the pitched ball. The force is completely balanced and results in a powerful outcome, often a home run.

In recent years the term has moved out of sports and into general use to mean that when competing forces meet at exactly the right time and place, it's a win-win for everyone. It's the best outcome between extremes.

So what is the sweet spot in life? I assume it varies with each of us, but all of us have our sweet spot—those moments we think of as absolute tranquility, deep peace, or utter satisfaction.

I've had those moments and so have most people. For example, I arrived the first time in Kenya in the middle of the night, spent the next two days in Nairobi, then left after dark to go upcountry, near the Kenya-Tanzania border. The following morning I awakened when the first rays of light crept into our room.

I went outside and stared at the countryside. I had never seen anything so beautiful. We were on the side of a mountain, and the sun was just peeping over another mountaintop. In the distance, a few cowbells punctuated the silence, but otherwise it was as if a new world had begun. That was a sweet spot for me.

Even after living there for several years, each morning I was able to get out at sunrise and watch that glorious event. It remained a sweet spot for me.

A sweet spot can be many things, and we probably all have more than one. But I have another sweet spot that I've enjoyed most of my adult life. I could call it by many names, such as a time for daily reflection, meditation, or prayer. It's my time to focus or refocus my day and straighten out the demands of the day.

I strongly advocate such a time, and we each need to find what works for us. For example, my friend's sweet spot is doing yoga. He sits in

> All of us have our sweet spot—those moments we think of as absolute tranquility, deep peace, or utter satisfaction.

silence and afterward speaks of being refreshed or invigorated. This exercise doesn't appeal to me, but it has calmed his anger.

I'd like to tell you a little about my sweet spot. When I became a serious Christian, I attended a church where they taught us that we need to pray daily. *Good idea*, I thought. But they did more: they spoke of being on our knees when we pray. Not a bad idea and I don't have any problems with that, but it simply never worked for me. Either I squirmed the entire time, or I fell asleep. It was a discipline I couldn't master.

Some years ago I began to run, and it was absolutely blissful. Yes, I huffed and puffed and strained for breath, and sometimes I felt that annoying stitch in my side. But it became a blissful time for me.

For the past thirty years I've found my sweet spot in running. Each morning I'm up around four thirty, regardless of the weather, and I run for forty-five minutes to an hour. I lose track of time. I'm in my bliss. Although vaguely aware of oncoming cars, I stay mainly on back streets.

The best part of the sweet spot is that something happens to me. I come back into the house tired, but at the same time I'm refreshed.

While I'm on the hoof, my mind is alert and I pray for other people—as I'm aware of their needs, I hold them up to God. I confess my failures, and sometimes I feel bad that I'm still making the same mistakes I made ten years ago. But I'm encouraged to know I'm at least aware and making progress.

There's also something else. Problems develop for which I can't figure out a solution, no matter how hard I try. I stop thinking about them until I go for my next run (or take time for an extra run). During the first part of my run, I avoid thinking about those concerns. About ten minutes before I arrive at home, my mind shifts to those unsolvable dilemmas, and almost as if unbidden, the solutions seem clear and obvious.

Years ago, a relative used to talk about sleeping on a problem and coming up with the answer after a good night's rest. Running does the same thing for me.

Running is my sweet spot. Ideas come to me. I see things differently. I know how to respond to a difficult person. In fact, this chapter and the previous one came out of a run this morning.

When I find my sweet spots,
I enjoy the bliss of life.

53

Living in the Flow

LIVING IN THE FLOW is a term I've heard for decades. And I know what it means because I've experienced it.

The best way I can describe being in the flow is to tell you how it works with me. It's becoming so caught up in what I'm doing or thinking that I'm aware of nothing else around me. If I'm typing, the words seem to gush from my fingers without any conscious input from my mind.

I concentrate so acutely on what I'm doing and remain oblivious to the noise, music, chaos, or activity around me.

I wish I could live in the flow during the conscious moments of my days, but that doesn't happen. And if I did, I would probably stop appreciating the value of the experience.

Some mornings when I run, I groan to myself about the weather or how tired I am. But once in a while—certainly not every day— I become aware that I've been pounding my feet against the asphalt for nearly an hour and I wasn't aware of it. I was lost in my thoughts, in cyberspace, in God's presence—I can use any of those terms.

Occasionally when I write, I get so engrossed that I feel as though no time has passed. Then I look up, and my office clock tells me it's been two hours.

The first time it happened to me I was still a pastor. I returned to my office after a particularly difficult session with an angry church member. I had about forty-five minutes between appointments, and an idea suddenly filled my mind. I began to type, and the words seemed to flow out of some deep, inner place. When I finished, perhaps seven minutes before my appointment, I read the entire piece and changed exactly one word.

I was amazed and deeply humbled to realize that it was good, and it had come through my fingers with seemingly no conscious input from me. I sold that article, and it was reprinted seventeen times. I even modified it slightly and used it as a chapter in one of my books.

Being in the flow works for me, and this unconscious pathway is open to all of us.

I'll give you one more illustration. I have a green thumb, and I make things grow easily. I simply do it.

For the past fifteen years I've liked turning off my computer around four o'clock in the afternoon (except in winter) and going outside to play in the yard. On my hands and knees with only clippers and a hand trowel, I start playing. (*It's not work.*) I have about three-quarters of an acre, and everything is hand-planted flowers or ground cover.

Down on my hands and knees, I'm alive in a world apart from the rest of creation. My mind keeps working, but I'm unaware of any mental activity. My whole being is involved and an hour passes, sometimes two, before my wife calls me or I awaken to my surroundings.

We need the flow. Our messy, unbalanced lives become richer and more creative if we learn to tap into it.

Finding our flow won't change the circumstances of our life, but it can enrich us where we are.

Our messy, unbalanced lives become richer and
more creative if we learn to tap into the flow.

54

Discovering
Our Bliss

MY FRIEND WILSON HELD A technical, high-level job with IBM. He detested going to work every day. He grumbled frequently about the conditions, the demands, and the structure.

"What do you really want to do with your life?" I asked. "What would make you truly happy?"

He said, "I'd like to write music."

"So why don't you do that?"

Wilson had a number of reasons—good, sensible, and practical ones—to explain why he just couldn't do it...at least not now.

About six months later, IBM announced they were moving Wilson's operation to Charlotte, North Carolina. He chose not to go with them.

"Now you can do what you've always wanted to do," I said.

He agreed but pointed out that he had a mortgage and a son still in high school. Within a month, Wilson had another job—very similar to what he had done for the past fourteen years. And he doesn't like the new job any better.

He hasn't written any music—at least not seriously. He took a few guitar lessons and plays occasionally.

"What now, Wilson?" I've asked several times since his son graduated from college. "Will you stay in your technical field? Or will you take risks and do what your heart says you want to do?"

So far, he's staying too busy with a list of reasons. He's miserable. Wilson has now hit the big 5-0 and I doubt he'll ever write music. Here's the reason: it's not his bliss. It's a dream, an ideal of what he thinks he would like.

In my opinion, Wilson doesn't want to write or play music. He wants to dream about a career in music.

And isn't that a little like most of us? We have dreams of what we *want* to do but when the opportunity comes, do we turn away from it?

By contrast, I want to tell you about Mark, who wanted to be a writer. He took a leave of absence for a year. "It's the only thing I love doing," he said. During his time away from the daily work world, Mark sold three e-zine articles and finished a novel. I haven't read it, but I doubt that it's good enough to sell.

We have dreams of what we *want*
to do but when the opportunity comes,
do we turn away from it?

Some of his friends have already chided him, "You've wasted a year of your life."

Mark laughs at that. "It's not the money. I'm finally doing something I've always wanted to do." He has plunged into writing.

"When I write, I feel alive. It's creative and I feel..." He searched for the word. "Happy. Contented. I don't know if I'll ever make a living at doing this. Probably not, but this is where my heart lies."

For Mark, writing is something he *must* do. It's like a compulsion.

He went back to his old position a few weeks ago. He says he puts in his thirty-eight-hour week and does the best job he can. "But in my free moments, I'm editing inside my head."

Mark has the right idea, and I'd like you to ask yourself three questions:

1. What's really ticking inside me?
2. What stirs that passion?
3. If finances were no problem, what would I do with my life?

You may be timid, insecure, untrained, or lacking in self-confidence, but something inside pushes you and refuses to let you rest. That's what I mean by bliss. It's knowing you are exactly where you want to be when you feel that deep tranquility—that bliss.

I first heard the phrase "Follow your bliss" on public television years ago when Bill Moyers did a six-hour interview with the late Joseph Campbell.

Campbell said there are two paths in life. He called the first the *right-handed path*. It's prudent and practical. He said that if we follow the right-handed path, it leads to the ladder of success. But if we climb the ladder of success, *we may learn that the ladder is against the wrong wall.*

Campbell spoke of the riskier *left-handed path.* He said it's the path of following our bliss, our rapture, or our ecstasy (his words).

He said that others might not understand our choice, and we have no guarantee to which wall our path will lead us, but if we choose the left-handed path, it is worth it *because the journey itself is its own reward.* When it happens, it shouts, "You've found your bliss!"

Our bliss may be as simple as cooking a meal, reading a book, or listening to music.

It's not what we do, but what it does to us.

If we discover our bliss—those things that pull us from the oppression of the urgent so we can focus on the power of the significant, those moments are a resurgence. It's like rebooting or recharging.

I'm following my bliss. I'm a writer because that's where I find my bliss. If I weren't writing, I'd be miserable. I'm extremely fortunate because I've found the job I love and I get paid for doing it.

I'm certainly not the only one. I talked to an accountant about a year ago and he said, "People think I'm crazy, but I love what I do." He talked about figures and numbers and the way he could help people. He went on longer than I wanted to listen, but I got it. He had found his bliss.

When I discover my bliss,
I discover wholeness.

55

Making It

Making it is a term we use often in the Western world. By that we mean being successful at whatever we do. But we usually mean even more. Most of the time it means we move upward while others fail.

"Everyone can't be a winner," we say. It's not so much that we want them to be defeated as it is that we want to succeed.

"That's the American way," I often hear. "Take care of number one." It sounds right, and it means we stay tightly focused on our goals and the things we yearn to achieve. Yet even we don't always make it. It's as if we're running a 10K and we stumble over an untied shoelace. Not only is the public embarrassment unacceptable, but it means we ruined our chance to be the first one to the finish line.

That's what we call conventional wisdom.

And I don't believe it.

If we truly want to make sense of life, one of the laws of the universe says: If we reach out to others, we're not losing ground and we're not failing. We're actually getting stronger. I can't explain how it works (although I know it does), but the more I help others, the more I end up helping myself.

When I was still in my teens I read a short story and don't even remember who wrote it. It was about three men trekking up dangerous mountains, probably the Himalayas, to reach a monastery. They encountered a sudden, powerful snowstorm that hindered their progress. They faced a narrow trail and darkness arrived before they reached the monastery.

One of them, who was much older, couldn't travel fast and was finally so exhausted he couldn't continue. The other two had to decide what to do.

> One of the laws of the universe says: If we reach out to others, we're not losing ground and we're not failing. We're actually getting stronger.

The leader of the group said, "Leave him. He'll slow us down, and we'll all die on the trail." He picked up his baggage and left.

The second man refused to abandon the old man but hoisted him onto his shoulder. He continued on the winding, upward trail. The temperature dropped, and the snow increased, but he kept on. He realized that he was going at only about half his pace, but he kept on.

About three hours later, the man with the burden stumbled over something and dropped the old man. As he started to get up, he realized he had tripped over the body of their leader. Dead. Frozen.

Not knowing what else to do, he picked up the old man again and continued to trudge upward. About fifty yards later he spotted the dim lights of the monastery. The two survived the ordeal.

The young man realized he had survived because he exerted his body, and the physical effort kept him from freezing.

I don't remember if it was a true story, and it doesn't matter. The lesson is simple: when I do what I can to help others, I help myself.

One of my favorite verses in the Bible, from the book of Proverbs, reads this way: "If you help the poor, you are lending to the

Lord—and he will repay you!"[10] For me, the poor refers to anyone in need—anyone I have the ability to go out of my way to help.

Ralph Waldo Emerson said it more poetically, but the principle is the same: "It is one of the most beautiful compensations of life that no man can sincerely try to help another without helping himself."

As a personal reflection on my life, I've tried to practice that principle. I haven't done it perfectly, and I've failed a few times. But it's still my ongoing goal. I've been fairly successful in my writing career. I've worked hard to learn the craft and to understand the publishing business— yet certainly no harder than others who haven't been as successful.

I believe God has smiled on me because of a commitment I made early in my writing career. By then I had met several writers whom I labeled *successful*. A few times I asked for help or advice. None of them responded—and they were people I knew rather well. One of them did say, "I don't train my competitors." (I never saw myself as his competitor, but obviously he viewed me that way.)

I promised God and myself that I would do whatever I could to help other writers make it. So I did what I could. And I continue to do what I can. That's as true as I know how to be. But it's more than doing what I could. I did what I could and then, as one of my friends puts it, "The Universe [I translate that to mean God] honored your giving."

I wouldn't say it his way, but I think he's right. I've achieved far more than I expected. I honored Proverbs 19:17, and God honored the principle in my life.

I do what I can to help others make it;
God does what He can to help me make it.

56

Living in the Afterward

I LIKE TO TALK AND WRITE about *afterward*—after we've made sense of life when it makes no sense. Rarely have I talked to anyone who went through deep trauma and confusion who didn't learn something from the ordeal.

- "I understand myself much better."
- "I grew as a person."
- "I'm more open to other people and their pain."
- "I'm stronger now."

But living in the messy now—right now—is the problem. We didn't ask for confusion or job loss, divorce, the ending of a relationship, a serious illness, or betrayal by a friend. We didn't ask, but we got them anyway.

When I was a pastor, I often heard people wail when their marriage or long-term relationship ended, with words like, "This is the worst thing that has ever happened to me."

Later—usually a year or two after the severe trauma—some of those same people told me that it turned out to be one of the best things that ever happened.

Perhaps that will be true with all of us, even though *afterward* is not the issue right now. I don't want to write about all the wonderful blessings of the future—although I believe the future can turn out better. I want to make sense of the craziness and grit of what's going on.

And yet *afterward* seems to lurk on the periphery of my vision. I may cry out that I don't care about what comes next—and in the darkest moments that's true. At the same time, because I know there *is* an afterward—a time when life gets better, my world improves, or God smiles on me—I keep going.

Because there is something beyond the pain and chaos, I persevere, sensing the best is still ahead. If I believed that life would never get better or that conditions wouldn't improve, I'm not sure how I would react.

A few years ago a friend named Wayne Smith took his own life. He faced an incurable disease and could see only darkness and despair ahead of him. Knowing that helps me understand why he did.

For Wayne there was no afterward. The terrible diagnosis and despairing words were the beginning of what lay ahead. And then it would get worse.

> Because there is something beyond the pain and chaos, I persevere, sensing the best is still ahead.

But in most situations, even in our deepest pain, we know it's not the end. We're sure life will continue. (We don't want people telling us that—we usually assume that's a kind of feel-good message for us so they can feel better themselves.)

Most of the time, though, life will get better, situations will improve, and we will learn and grow from this experience.

Today isn't good; tomorrow may be worse. But afterward—after this is over—I will be stronger.

57

Between Principles and Values

"Principles remain, but values change," my friend Barry Spencer said recently, and after he explained, I agreed with him.

We build our lives on principles. Those are the standards that dictate our lives. Sometimes they're consciously thought through, sometimes our parents, teachers, or contemporaries instilled them.

Stan Cottrell grew up in Kentucky. Frequently he would refer to the "code of the hills." He used that in referring to reaching out to and caring for friends. "We take care of family—and family means those we care about," he once said.

More than twenty years later, our house burned and we lost everything. The insurance company put us into a motel, and we had to get a ride from someone to get there. About an hour after we checked in, the hotel phone rang.

"This is Stan," he said. He told us he had seen the report of the fire on TV. "I'll come and get you in the morning, and you'll stay with Carol and me until you have a place to live."

I thanked him and politely refused.

"This is not negotiable," Stan said. "The code of the hills says we take care of our own."

His words touched me, and I couldn't refuse. That was a principle by which Stan lived. As much as anything, it told me about who he is. He's now in his sixties, but the principle is still part of him.

Principles don't change; values do. I need only think of the changes in attitudes during the past half century. Thirty years ago, for instance, no principled woman wore pants or slacks to church, weddings, or funerals. And none went to any formal occasion without wearing a hat. No man dared to enter those places without a tie and jacket. That generation lived by the principle that those events are special and wanted to honor the occasion. They expressed their values by the clothes they wore.

Principles don't change; values do.

Last Sunday I sat in a church service with about 125 people. I was the only male in the building wearing a tie and jacket (and that included the pastor). Only two women wore dresses. Values have changed.

Here's another example. When I was in grade school I once said to a classmate, "What the devil should I do?" The teacher overheard me and reprimanded me for swearing. I didn't understand how she could consider that foul language. Certainly no one would today.

Or here's another place where values have shifted. The King James Version of the Bible appeared in 1611. Eight times the translators used the word *piss* for urinating. By the time I came along in history, refined people called the word vulgar, even though it is again slipping into common usage.

What do these examples mean? We have underlying principles— they're the rarely changing parts of ourselves that we violate only at great inner pain. One of the principles of my life is the golden rule— treating others as I wish them to treat me. Sometimes I treat others badly, but when I become aware of it, my conscience troubles me, and guilt hovers over me.

But, as I've shown above, my values shift. So that leaves me with a question. Are the people of today less committed to their ideals and standards than a previous generation?

That's a general question, but my answer is simple: they hold to the important codes of life, but their manner of expressing those principles has changed.

As we struggle with the messiness of life, maybe we're confusing values and principles.

Life makes little sense
unless I hold to principles
and remain open to rethink my values.

58

We're Not Who We Used to Be

"The most profound spiritual changes often take place when we're least aware of them." I read those words recently on a website. I think they're true.

You may want to think of them as inner changes. That means we become different, better, stronger, and more the person we'll eventually become.

Another way to put this is that we grow. Sometimes we burst through barriers and race forward; at other times we stagger through the barricades. Regardless of how, we do get through them. And we're different after we reach the other side.

Usually in the midst of chaos, people cry out, "God, just get me out of this mess."

When we hurt or life turns chaotic, we seem able to focus only on the rigors of life, the unfairness of our situation, or our anxieties over how we're going to pay the mortgage this month.

When life gets messy and doesn't make sense, something goes on inside us, and that "something" is probably an inner force of which we're unaware. We're learning and we're maturing, but it doesn't feel like it.

But we also reach the place where we feel as if we've struggled enough. "I'm tired of this," we say. "How much longer will this go on?" In the Bible the psalmist cried out, "Oh, Lord, how long will you forget me? Forever? How long will you look the other way?"[11]

When we encounter another of life's inevitable messes, we don't stay in the same place. We change. If we refuse to respond, the situation usually makes the decision for us.

We can fight and refuse to allow tragedy or pain to conquer us. Quite frequently I receive requests from people who want to hire me to write their story. I was amazed at the stamina and determination of a high school boy who wasn't expected to walk but insisted that he would not only walk but play football again (and he has). I heard from a man blinded in an accident, yet he scales mountains.

But there are always those who give up without much effort. They groan and never move beyond seeing the unfairness of life.

Regardless, none of us is the same after a crisis. Even if we surrender, we solidify and strengthen ourselves some after that depressive mode. If we keep getting up each time we're kicked down, we move beyond the not-making-sense part of life. Afterward—after we've moved on—we look back and realize that we're not the way we were.

None of us is the same after a crisis.

We have changed. We were so focused on the battle (or the lack of it) that we had no awareness of what was happening to us internally. What goes on inside us is that we have experienced a problem, and we chose a mode of response. That decision, especially if it was a good one, enables us to face the next one.

That's how life works. As we face challenges or problems of any kind—*and I mean face them*—we survive and grow *because of* the experience. It's like going through school. We have to finish one grade before we're ready for the next.

One of my friends said recently, "I love to admire my flowers in the sunshine, but they also need the darkness to grow."

I'm not who I used to be, and I don't know who I'll be at the end of my life. I'm a work in progress.

Notes

1. Jan Kuzma and Cecil Murphey, *Live 10 Healthy Years Longer* (Nashville, Tenn.: Word Publishing, 2000).

2. Don Piper with Cecil Murphey, *90 Minutes in Heaven* (Grand Rapids, Mich.: Revell, 2004), 17.

3. Matthew 6:27

4. 1 Timothy 6:6–8

5. Philippians 4:11–12

6. Genesis 50:18

7. Genesis 50:19–21

8. Romans 7:19

9. Matthew 5:43–44

10. Proverbs 19:17

11. Psalm 13:1

Acknowledgments

My sincere thanks to individuals who make life difficult for me (and I won't name them). Regardless of their intentions, they push me to examine areas of my life that I would have preferred to ignore.

I appreciate Jason Rovenstine, Carlton Garborg, and Ramona Tucker of Summerside. I *know* I'm in good hands with you.

I especially acknowledge my assistant, Twila Belk, and my literary agent, Deidre Knight. They claim that they're the wind beneath my wings. That's probably true.

David Morgan has been a significant part of my life for three decades and has talked with me through much of this material.

This is to acknowledge my love to Wanda and Randy, Cecile, and John Mark and Cathie.

But most of all, thank you, Shirley, for loving me, for being my wife, and because you're the best person I know.

About the Author

Cecil (Cec) Murphey has written or co-written more than 120 books, including the *New York Times'* best seller *90 Minutes in Heaven* (with Don Piper) and *Gifted Hands: The Ben Carson Story* (with Dr. Ben Carson). His books have sold millions and have brought hope and encouragement to readers around the world.

OTHER BOOKS BY CECIL MURPHEY INCLUDE:

Getting to Heaven: Departing Instructions for Your Life Now (with Don Piper)

Knowing God, Knowing Myself

When a Man You Love Was Abused

Hope and Comfort for Every Season

Words of Comfort for Times of Loss

Christmas Miracles

When God Turned Off the Lights

When Someone You Love Has Cancer

Everybody's Suspect in Georgia (fiction)

I Choose to Stay and *Immortality of Influence* (with Salome Thomas-EL)

Rebel with a Cause (with Franklin Graham)

Cecil Murphey enjoys speaking for churches and for
events nationwide. For more information, or to
contact him, visit his website at www.cecilmurphey.com.

Cecil's blog for male survivors of sexual abuse:
www.menshatteringthesilence.blogspot.com.

Cecil's blog for writers:
www.cecwritertowriter.com.